T0193341

A Practical Guide to Life

BALBOA.
PRESS

A DIVISION OF HAY HOUSE

Balboa Press books may be ordered through booksellers or by contacting:

Balboa Press
A Division of Hay House
1663 Liberty Drive
Bloomington, IN 47403
www.balboapress.com
1 (877) 407-4847

Print information available on the last page.

ISBN: 978-1-9822-0118-0 (sc)
ISBN: 978-1-9822-0120-3 (hc)
ISBN: 978-1-9822-0119-7 (e)

Library of Congress Control Number: 2018903808

Balboa Press rev. date: 05/16/2018

From GOD:

For it is written. We the people do declare that this so called bible be it written to do the work for the people, by the people, in the name of G-D. For I am G-D of all the people. For it is written. I command thee to honor me as it is written. The love I share is all for you. I have been here for you always. Look inside. The heart that beats is you AND me. We are one. One beat. One breath. Together we are one.

On this day we beat as one. Together we will conquer. Trust in me as I trust in you. Like the waves that come in crash and move on. We come together as the waves hit and split.

It is time to know the truth, for we are here together to become greater human beings. Together we are great. A great people. Like the song "Broken Wings" says. "Take these broken wings and learn to fly again." We are one. One person. One world. For we are all connected. Connected in the outer world. The world of love to do great things. The power is in us. For to move forward we need each other *all* the time. Not occasionally. Together we can do it. Look inside. Feel you're beating heart. Touch it.

Know it is me. Listen … Speak my name. For I am your G-D. I am you. I can't stress that enough. The tapestry we weave together to become one. One soul, one love, one being. Here me O Israel. Here me speak. My word is your command. I tell you this for it is so. It is like we are beating as one.

Our son hollow his name. Below we find our song in heaven, it is so. I call you this day to believe in me for it is so. I bring you this daily bread. The bread of happiness, of love and caring. For I take not a piece of this bread. I share it amongst my children of the sun. You shine forth. You are the light. The shiny stars. The light within. I love you all. You are my children. My flowers in the garden. For it is written with love.

Remember this always. We lie together to become one. As I mentioned earlier, one beating heart. One soul. As one for always. I put the breath of me into you. You are my beating heart.

Let's begin again this time to remember as I say. For it is written.

My child beneath the sun, as we glow we rise. Follow the sun. Follow the warmth. Follow your breath, your beating heart. As one, I give this to you. Take it with you. Our daily bread. Spread it like butter. Spread your wings. Reach the sky. Hear me roar, even louder than before. For these are my words. I guide you this day.

As the sand washes over me. I clear the dirt. As I move you forward. One step at a time. It is time to clear up the dirty waters. Wash it anew. Begin a new dawn. Remember, we are one, one beating heart.

You are my child. My love, my soul. My daily bread. I love all of you dearly. We begin our lesson today from the heart. I give you this from the depth of my soul to yours. You are mine. As once I said before, take me in your hands. Rub your soul. Caress your soul and you will understand. For we are one. I want you to believe for it is so. My words. My commands. Become as one for I love you so. Take these words as I command you today. Rub them on your body. Make them as your daily routine. For they should be with you every day, every minute. To surround you with the tapestry of love.

My child, my son, my daughter, you are me and I am you. I feel the warmth of your soul and the warmth of your heart. *We beat as one.*

I hear you roar. I hear your prayers. As I try to answer you all, I feel your pain. I hear your words. I can't take the pain away for it is time to learn. Time to become the lesson of love. Always find it within. Pull it out of your inner most wisdom, the heart. Find it in your feet, find it in the sun, and the ground. Hear it in the wind. It blows all around you. I encircle you with it every day.

Don't worry about the pain. I only give you what you can handle. Taste it, caress it, and make it yours. Be proud of it. It will be gone before you know it. Like a wave moves on the shore, breaks, spreads and moves back out, just to meet another wave to rise up, break and move out once again. We are always moving, changing, and growing. For it is so. Remember the wind. It moves all around us, constantly changing directions. Sometimes it is strong while other times it is barely there. But always there even when you don't know it is around. For I love you so.

Here me roar for you are my child. I made you. You are me. As the morning sun shines look up to the sun, see me in your reflection. The time has come for you to believe in me. Take my reflection in the sand and see me in you.

Look deep inside, pull through your guts. Yes the ugly as well as the beautiful parts. I love your limbs, your hands, and your hearts. Remember we are the same. Look into the sky. See me. We are one once again. Look into the morning sun, see me, and feel me. Hear me roar. I am here in your heart, your lungs, even your ears. I listen to your prayers, your hopes and your dreams. You think I don't listen but I do. I do hear you always. Sometimes it is best the way it is progressing. Sometimes not and that is when I step in. Remember you have the power to change, to control what is happening. It is inside you because we are one. The light inside. As I guide you to the falls in the depths of despair. Remember this. You are not alone. I am there to catch you. I might watch you fall some, just to see if you will begin to fly. So in those dark moments spread your wings and learn to fly again.

Remember even in the darkest of time. I will always catch you. I will not let you drop to the bottom. You are me and I you. I don't like to see you hurt your beautiful soul. For when you fly look down as you spread your wings. See those below scoop them up, help each other, for we are one. Show them your wings. Let them touch them. Feel their softness, smell them, and caress them for they are mine. We will always fly together amongst the angles of the sky. So soar, flap those wings. Listen to them in the wind while looking down so you don't crash deep below the edge of life. Stay with me, listen inside. I will teach you to fly *all* of you! Trust in me. Show them (the angles) your love. Feel your heart beat as one. I love you all. ALL my children. All races. All colors. All heights. For we are one. I know I keep repeating this but it is important for you to understand. This is an important point to get. I want to stress this. We have fought in wars, been in hard times and it is time we merge as one beating heart. I want you to love one another as you love yourself. The energy when we come together is stronger than when we stand alone. I'm tired of seeing you fight, steal, and decimate. Put down your guns, your swords, your bombs. Be at peace. For when you are at peace we see clearly.

When we open our eyes we can learn to love. Love is the answer to all. Love can carry us through dark times. It can raise us higher. It is strong. You think the dark times are heavy and strong but that is wrong. Love is wonderful. Listen, it is all around. Close your eyes now and take a moment. Fill your lungs with love, breath out. Blow it out. Spread the love. Don't worry about germs. Love will never get you sick. Feel the release inside you as you blow, feel your body relax. Do this often. Notice the people around you let their guard down and relax with you. This is all it takes to reduce the tension in the room. Try it, try it now. For we are one. As you do this throughout the day your brain waves stretch out. Thus your mind can think more clearly. Your body will relax, your muscles will go limp but supple. Your lungs will feel the warmth. Feel it through your veins.

LESSON 1

I gather you here today to learn the lesson of perseverance. It is a lesson particularly in 2 parts. One, to do it correctly is to be conscious of the love you have for yourself. If there is no self-love you can't have patience. It's all about the quality of love you have for yourself. To be totally centered and in tune with your soul. Then and only then can you have patience for others. To give of yourself is to love yourself first and then you can enjoy other souls. To become patient with your neighbors, look inside. What do you see? Do you see despair and thus no room for anyone else? Or do you see light and movement inside? The ability to open yourself up for patience requires room in your heart. In order to give of yourself, there must be room in your soul. Cast away the darkness by this prayer.

"Hallow my name for my soul is light. Be thy name. Mark me in your heart. Hold me there. Let thy light caress my soul. Be my mother and father. Give me the strength to push the darkness away. Amen.

Be thy daughter and son. Hold me tight for I am within. I am with you always. Push that darkness away. Know I am with you always. Amen."

Now look inside, do you still see darkness? Or do you see the light? Look at your heart. Is there more love? If so spread the word, help your fellow man. Give of yourself. For my will is yours. Be patient. Show your love. Show your spirit. Be awake. Open your eyes, look around. Is there someone who needs your aid? Go to them and do my work. You will be rewarded. Give of yourself. Help my children of the light. Cast out the darkness and do my will.

For to have patience is to have the act of kindness, for yourself and your fellow man. Be strong. Be love. I am your savor and you are mine.

Open your book, turn to page 62. Look at it quickly, glance down. What do you see? Do you see the word patience? It's there. Look hard. Study it. Pay attention to the shape. Know that shape, every curve, every angle is you. Memorize it. Hold it to your heart. Caress it.

LESSON 2

Part two of patience. The act of War. War – the act of fighting either within or with our fellow human beings. It was there since the beginning of time and it will be there tomorrow. There is no way getting around it. I know it is not possible to cast that away. But know it is wrong, just understand it. Make it yours by showing understanding and patience. War is the lack of understanding and patience. A lack of love. Be thy will. Unfortunately, it will always be there. From that first burst of light it has been there. It is part of man. It is part of the lessons of life. Try to understand both sides. For knowledge is freedom and freedom is love and patience. There is a time for right and wrong. A time to argue, a time to yell and a time to make love. Learn what you can. Read, watch your TV. Understand what's happening around you but don't get to close. Just learn. Except for all the men and women out there on the front line. For that is my will. Be all you can. Show your patience. Understand there will always be fighting. Do what you can and move on. Take the cycle of life. Understand mankind. For freedom to last there must be conflict.

I know that is not what you want to hear. But for every kindness, there will always be conflict. The good and the bad. I would prefer it to not be so, however I know it will be. We need conflict to show our power and our strength, even if man gets hurt. Understand this power and the ability to show ones muscle is a part of some people's justification to live. That is who they are in their journey, their mission. If you can rise above it. Great. But I'm not foolish. Some of you will not. I understand. I want others to feel your pain, caress it and just understand. Because that is the way of the world. Do thy will and know that the darkness and light will never come together.

It is the piece we long for. The joy of living in harmony. The happiness of coherent love. But don't be fooled. I cannot give you this. It is not to be. I want harmony, joy and happiness in the best way possible. That way must be inside you. Look inside to find the ecstasy within. I am your joy, love and harmony. For we are one. One love. Even those in darkness, I love you all. You are me.

The room you make inside for patience is the room I need for you to find me. The answer is love, for I am love.

"Be thy will and thy will be done"

Repeat that saying over and over when you feel the darkness and know I am with you. Unfortunately unfavorable things will happen but know that the future depends on it. The long term vision is working for the divine. You in this dimension cannot see it but rest assured I can. The best outcome will emerge in time. Grasp it, know it. Thy will be done.

The wars, the conflicts and clashes will never be escaped. If you need to hide so be it. But don't disappear. Remember even in your deepest sorrow, I am there. We will emerge with the greatest of joy.

I love you all. I want all of you to understand my love. I have seen your hate and your cruelty. That is not what I desire. Be thy will. Love thy will. With your breath, blow the love. I challenge you this. We need more love. Picture this image. Be that image. Drown my sorrow, cover it with love my children. For you all are my sons and daughters. It is time to believe every one of you is special!!! Not just the disciples. You are all the same. I do NOT love one more than the other. Hold out your hands. Cup them so you can fill your cup with the energy of love. Fill my weight, raise the cups up. Embrace my love. Look to the stars. Relish in their beauty for we are one. One universe. One sparkling star in the galaxy of love. Hold my heart within yours. Try to find the light. Breath. Be mine.

Open your heart. Love your neighbors as me. Drink it in. Love is always the answer because I tell you so.

Let the juices flow. Open your hearts. Hold thy neighbor. Become one. For the love abounds us. Stretch to the stars. Remember to look up.

LESSON 3

Fear not for I am with you. The opposite of fear is the unbounding love I have for you. Take the shadow of fear. Embrace it for there will be times it comes and goes. Talk about it. Don't keep it inside. Let your brothers and sisters help. We are here together as one. Take that knowledge. Get the help you need. Open your arms, grasp for your brothers and sisters. You might not know what to do but they do. Open your mind to the power of others. Their experience in life can help you. Don't stand alone in a tight cocoon. Open that rope. Bend in the wind. Having fear is a lesson. It tells you to open your mind. Research what can be done. Open the books. Ask for help. If you seek you will find the love you need for happiness.

We seek relationships. It is part of our soul desires. To be together as one. Don't stand alone. We are all family. Check on a friend daily. Share your love. And you will notice some of your fears will disappear. For when we share our love a certain blanket comes over us and makes a fear seem not so bad after all. But don't be fake and do this because I say to. Truly care and open your hearts. Make sure you truly feel it. I will know the difference. If you don't, stop and smell the flowers. Think about things. In time you will know what to do. I challenge you this.

Be of service when the time is right. Just like when you had fear, you reached out for help. Return that love. Help those in need. We all go through different waves at different times. In the ocean of life we rise and fall differently. Take those who run with the tide, bring them back out with you so they can rise with a big wave as you do. The peaks and valleys gush through time. Float with them.

I am your savor. Your creator. Remember we are one. Take my hand as we walk in the valley of the sun.

LESSON 4

Repent – when things go wrong and they will. Ask for forgiveness. No one is perfect. As a human we make mistakes, do harm to thy neighbors or possibly say the wrong things. Hear no evil. And yet we are tempted. Rest assured I judge not. For I made you and understand when things falter. All I ask is you do your best. When things are not perfect just apologize. Find a way to make amends. Open the door to your heart. Look inside. Do you see mostly evil (we all have some) or do you see mostly love. If you see evil. Pray.

"I am the creator of me. I choose no evil. I choose no harm. For we are one. Amen"

Take the evil and push it away. Bring in the beauty of life. Caress it on your soul. If when you look inside and you see mostly love or even if you don't, know I'm smiling down at you. I love my children. I judge not.

LESSON 5

In the book of life, there are many characters. Some strong. Some weak. Some smart. And some challenged. Embrace all. We all have special gifts to share. Don't look at the amount of money one has or the lack there of. You all come into this life naked, cold and wet. You leave the same. Some lives are rich with love and some with coins. But know you are all the same. Share what you have. Open your purse, your wallet and give aid to those who need it.

For my child with the biggest of heart - you – expand that wealth. Be there for your neighbor. Listen to their troubles. It is not necessary to always offer advice. There are days your fellow brother and sister just want to know you care. Show them respect and they will respect you back. Give them a hand and know that is me. You work my magic. We all have the power to create. To give and to express joy. Joy is one of my favorite things. It creates many things. For it is all about love and being of service.

When we don't feel well it is hard to open our arms and minds. Take care of yourselves first! Do what you need to find that joy. Only then can we give of ourselves. Be thy own teacher first.

For you see taking care of yourselves first means being your own mother or father or even teacher. Taking care of your own soul first is the most important way to show your love. How can you have love for others if you can't wrap yourselves first? The love you hold inside can only spread with the foundation built inside.

Take the grounding of this foundation seriously. Nurture this growth or these roots by reading, sleeping, eating well, and by wrapping yourself in the blanket of love. We are our greatest creator. Be thy will and thy will be done. (*My favorite saying*).

LESSON 6

I hold thy heart near. Arguments can and will erupt. Stand up for yourself but don't explode. Listen to each other. See their side before you explode. Learn why they are saying what they believe. Understand it. It is never a one way road. I'm not saying allow someone to roll over you. Stand your ground politically. Roll it around. Rest assured at times you are both right.

Conflict can be seen in many ways. There can be evil or darkness. However this is not the only conflict around. It can be as gentle as saying a color looks or holds a different hue. For we all see things in a different way. Respect that. That is the way to loving thy neighbor. Don't hold your thoughts or feelings inside. It will only foster resentment, hatred and a dismay that will only grow. Green can look many different ways. Who is to say which one is right? I for one don't know so how can you?

I prefer to look at the sky and clouds. Take that image and find different things in the clouds. Ask your neighbor what they see. Let them describe their image. And therefore with greater knowledge you can draw the bigger picture. Sometimes that requires taking time to do research. Hold your thought for the count of five before the explosion begins. I realize it isn't always easy. But remember my idea of the cloud. Breathe and then release your thoughts. Try to stay calm. Listen to their side and explain yours. I have seen some of you throw things, grab things and show your guns in the heat of the moment. That is not the way to love. If things get too heated walk away!! Save your soul. Don't let the evil in. Do thy will.

Evil is all around us. By having a strong foundation of love it cannot get in. I must say a few words about evil. I know some of you worry and think about it often. I created evil to give the good times more joy. Life would be boring and without appreciation. Try to understand, I do things out of love. For everything is a lesson. A way to grow. Sometimes it is a lesson for history. To learn. To remember so you don't keep doing the same wrong things. Unfortunately at times I have to make a rather large point to get my message across. Forgive me if you have lost a loved one during that time, but know they are always with you. Try to see the lesson which is always for the greater good. Evil can be strong. Hold tight. Just when you think the boat is going to tip in the waves of life. Look around. I will always throw a life line out. Open your eyes and take hold. This works for large conflicts as well as small. Try to observe what is happening. Look for a lesson. Take the fear you are feeling and look inside. What does that fear say? Can you remember something this conflict reminds you of? Or maybe it is something you are afraid to stand up to. Sometimes there is no way to see the other side and you have to run away. Don't feel the only way is to stay and hold your ground. There are times the lesson is to get away and know you are capable on your own. Not all minds can come together. Be strong and know when to fold. That is the greatest of love for yourself you can do. You will have learned a great lesson. Be aware of what is happening or I will give it to you again and again till you get it. Even when you think you understand it, I might make sure you do and throw it at you once again for one last time.

Remember that at times my point of evil must be driven home, even in the most horrific of times. Everything under the sun is a lesson for that is how you grow.

Let it be. That is so.

Lesson 7

I have mentioned we are one. This is important. Remember this. When you feel joy or disappointment it will comfort you and take you far. We create together. The lessons you learn are with me too. We do it together as one. There are times you are in the neutral zone. Things are going marvelous. You are coasting in the sun. And then bang. Something happens. Stop and think about the people around you. What did you reflect? What image of them has mirrored or reflected this response? What thoughts are in your head? Since we are all one, our actions, our thoughts, our emotions show up in our neighbors. Be aware. Stop and think what possibility could have caused this. For example, if hatred for a friend is on your mind, look to your left and then to your right, is someone showing distain for you or a fellow neighbor? What you think and say affects others.

That is why love is so important. When you have love in your heart you will reflect that back out to your companions. If you have fear or hatred that is what you will find. For the universe seems immense but it is not. It is actually small and beautiful. Look at a rock. Really look at it. Does this remind you of anyone? Hold this rock to your heart. Do you want to be hard, solid and non-conforming? Or do you want to feel soft and subtle? Or better yet look in a mirror. What do you see? Can you see the love emanating from you? Look at your eyes. Do they sparkle? Are they bright or do they sink in? When you feel hate, ask yourself is this what G-D would do? Judge not. Be as one. Remember I love all my children. All colors, shapes and sizes. Hate not, fear not, for we are one. Take my hand, together we can change the world. For I love you all.

LESSON 8

When you see a blade of grass blowing in the wind. What do you smell or see? Do you see one of my greatest creations? Feel the blade of grass between your toes. Does it feel sharp and itchy? Or does it feel sticky or soft? In this lesson of love I want you learn about patience. It is like the blade of grass. It bends in the wind. Think of it as a carpet for the universe. You are all blades of grass. At times it feels like someone steps on you and flattens you out. But when you least expect it you pop back up. No one can step on just one blade without affecting others. It is always in a group. You need each other. Be the first to pop back or help someone else up, and out of default you will stand back up too. There are times when you must think of your neighbor first. They need you. Hold out your hand.

LESSON 9

Archangel Uriel comments

One day an earth quake will come. Shake your life as you have never known it. It will ricochet in the depths of your soul. Since you are human know that mercy is with you. I am mercy. Like the blade of grass G-D talked about, you will bounce back. Be that mercy. Help others and they will help you. Take their kindness and impress it on your soul. There will be a time you will use it on someone else. Remember this always. Our children are watching and learning.

When I was a boy. Yes I was small once upon a time. In some ways things were so much larger. I would watch the kindness of others. It would take time for me to learn what I wanted to keep inside and to discern what was best brushed aside or spoken out loud. I would take the kindness of knowledge and store it in my memory. Remember the eyes of souls are upon you, watching and learning. Your actions do not go unnoticed. Your actions will live on forever. You have the ability to be a great teacher. Help your children cross the streets. Allow them to cross completely safe and with comfort. The other side is as grand as the side they are currently on.

I remember a time when such an event was scary. I didn't like being there. I watched the grownups react. I learned from them. And now I help you merge as a kind adult.

However for those adults who are not as kind, stop the beatings, the swearing, and the abuse! Ask for help. Don't let what happened to you go on forever. The abuse is <u>not</u> what I or G-D want. Yes sometimes this abuse makes our children strong adults, but usually the violence continues on from life time to life time.

We beg you to end this now. Be strong, reach out your hand. In the depths of your soul pull the evil out. Take my hand. Ask your neighbors to reteach your soul. I know you can do it. Be patient with yourself. It will take time. You didn't learn this tragedy overnight and thus you can't expect the goodness to emerge without some effort and patience. This I know is so.

In the trash of society we take our children to the bowels of the beast. Try to learn from your experience and break the pattern. Society needs to be better. Trust we are with you. Take our hand. Know we are one. Pull yourself out of the beast. Even though we are one; you have to do the work. Pray to me but ask for help. You cannot do this alone. We love you. My brother and my sister, do it now.

Lesson 10

GOD is back

Take my hand as we cross the valley of your souls. Know we are one and have the ability to create what we want our lives to be. Watch your thoughts. They become your beliefs and your actions. Your thoughts manifest into what you were thinking. So if you immerse your reality into something you fear. Rest assured it will happen. If you think of only love and safety then that will happen. If you dream or worry of lack – lack of health, lack of gold coins etc. Then you will receive just that. Imagine your life – close your eyes and focus on something good, something grand. See yourself with it. Feel what it would be like to have what you dream. Smell it. Gather all your senses. Immerse yourself into that belief.

I can give you everything you ever imagined. Don't focus on the lack there of. Remember the love, the abundance. You can all have everything you desire.

LESSON 11

I take you this day into my heart. Where the grass is green and the sky is blue. I hold all of you close. Be patient, wise and loyal. Know there is only one G-D, one almighty, one knower of all. I opened the ocean for you. I showed you the burning bush and now I show you my deepest desires. We have come a long way. However it is time for *more*. More love! More understanding of our neighbors. More compassion. Take me. Know we are one!! Hold me. Together we can clean the dirt. It's time to make things even greater. Listen to my words as I command you this day. Engrave them on your posts. Make them yours. For you are me. My son and daughter.

Know I hear your prayers. I do listen. Keep me close. Open your ears. Hear me roar. Follow my commandments. For this is the only way. I love you always.

LESSON 12

Yes, I hear you. I hear you loud and clear. It may seem like I'm not listening but I am. I'm in your thoughts, your actions. What you do, we all do together! We create together. Remember we are one. Everyone has a piece of me inside. Take your thoughts for example. Ever wonder why you thought something? Or for some unexplained reason you had to walk down a particular street. That is me or your guides moving you in a direction. Sometimes we do this to introduce you to a new neighbor or perhaps we want you to learn a new lesson. Either way, always follow your gut. Know we are "talking" to you. Moving you in a particular direction for a special reason.

Now there are several different kinds of thoughts. For one, the one we just talked about. And then there are the ones you are creating your future with. Your minds are very powerful. They control everything! Your thoughts also tell us what you want in life. For example, you may think you just don't have enough gold coins. And you need more to pay your bills. What you are really saying is you like the feeling of lack. The worrying, the constant concern of all the bills coming in give you something to concern yourself with. Some of you thrive on worry. I actually think you enjoy it. Stop it now! Believe in me. Most of the time I will provide. However, there are a few cases that I won't. Because I may need you to learn a lesson. For instance, maybe you spend your coins on things that are not best for you, like drugs or alcohol. Or maybe we are trying to teach you to budget your finances. Either take action and change things or trust you have *plenty* of gold coins.

Be careful of the thoughts of lack. They can do a lot of damage.

"I am rich. I have all my needs meant."

Repeat that often. Change your thoughts. Feel it, be it, hold it to your heart.

Your thoughts and your feelings create your values and your beliefs. Watch them. Pay attention. Write them down. Be aware of what you are creating. Either we are creating a lesson or you are creating an event. I can't stress this enough! Don't go through life half asleep. Open your hearts and your eyes. Pay attention to your world. It will make a difference.

If you think the world has a lot of people to mistrust and are evil, then that is what you will create. So when you open your eyes, stop and think why these things are happening to you. Take a minute to go within. Take an honest look at yourself. What have you been thinking? If you think there is nothing but loving people then that is what you will find. If you think your neighbors want to hurt you then that is what you will get. Be mindful.

Fill your boat with love and abundance. This vessel is flexible. It will keep expanding. Don't shrink it down.

Lesson 13

It is said we are strong people. We are wise and caring. Then tell me this. Why do you pilfer and rumble through your neighbors' things? Why do you take that which is not yours? Do you feel you *deserve* that which is not yours? **Deserve** that's the word for today. I don't like that word. No one deserves anything!! Especially if you did not purchase it with your own coins. I command you this day. STOP the pilfering! Do the right thing by your neighbor. No one deserves to have their home destroyed or their place of business. People work hard to have the things they have. It makes me sad when I see my sons and daughters take that which is not theirs. I implore you to stop this madness. You do not deserve these things. You deserve nothing!

From the beginning of time I have witnessed this. I even engraved it in stone for you to stop and yet it continues. Remember this as I command you once again. You do not deserve anything!! Do not take that which is not yours! When you feel the urge stop and remember my words. Yes we are strong. Use that strength to earn your own coins. Have respect for your neighbor's possessions. Be kind, gracious and humble.

That brings me to the other side of the coin. Those who have many things. Don't flaunt what you have. Don't wave your things in others faces. It is great if you have worked hard and been able to produce these items. I have nothing against that. But I do despise showing off your wears. Keep it simple and hidden. If you are so abundant than share the wealth among your neighbors. I have asked this of you for so long now. And yet have seen so little of it. I would like to see more. I am not talking about giving for a tax credit. Or to a politician who will promote something you stand for. I am talking truly a release of funds to someone who has none. Not everyone can be as blessed with their coins. Some are learning lessons of lack and when they get a blanket or a hot meal my heart glows. There will be times you all will be in need. Maybe not this lifetime but surly next. Remember this and give of your heart.

LESSON 14

Other lifetimes. Yes I am saying it. Reincarnation exists. You all have had many lives and many more to come. And different beliefs depending on which life you are in. I did not create you to die, to be washed away in the sand. I created you to learn. To be the best you can be. One lifetime would not do it. Each lifetime represents a lesson, (for some many lessons). For example, if you fear gays than your next life you will come back as a gay man. My goal is for you to love <u>all</u> man, woman and child. Don't fear that which you don't understand. Embrace it. All man is equal in my eyes. All colors of skin have the same color of blood. I'm even talking about those who have weight, speaking, seeing, hearing, walking and dressing issues. You all have your own journey. Don't fear. You are all near to me in this life and next. Pay attention to whom you dislike. For you will be them in your next adventure. That I promise you. My will be done. I love you all just the way you are.

The bible should not say you have to be a straight or heterosexual male or female. Someone changed my words to fit their need or desire. I command you this day, look into your neighbors' eyes. Really look. See their souls. Look for the good. I know it is there. We are all the same deep down. All on different trains of learning and striving for acceptance. We need each other. Respect their journey. Accept them. Be them. For we are one. My children of the sun.

LESSON 15

As I take you down this new road of purity, I know for some of you this information may sound strange or even unbelievable. While others have known this information in their hearts for a long time. Rest assured it is time to know my truth. You have all been studying things that have not been completely accurate. Trust in this book for G-D is my witness.

I give you this at this time because you are ready. The time is right. Until now I did not feel you needed to know or could handle what I wanted to convey. This book is the truth. The only truth you need to know.

Get in your boat of love. Fill it with all your most cherished memories. And know I am there with you. So is Jesus, Archangels Michael, Gabriel, Raphael, Shmuel, Uriel, and Ezekiel. We are all with you. We surround you with our love, compassion and honor. Feel our solute. We feel your pain and your fear. Wash those feeling away. Fill your boat with love, for love is the answer. It will always make you better. For this is so.

LESSON 16

When things are tough or when we feel despair; Look at the sky. Know I'm with you. Put down your guns, drugs and bad words. Look at your neighbor that is making you so upset. What color are their eyes? Really look at them. Breathe. Just breathe. Understand we all believe in different things. Don't judge them. If it is not what you choose know that's ok. Your way isn't always correct and neither is theirs! Trust me, I see it all. Look at the other side and if you need to walk away than do. Glory is there for you.

I will show you the way. Put down your idols. I'm here inside you. Not on an altar. Not at a crop. Not in a book or in a stall. Hold your hand to your heart. Feel it beat. Just as you know you are alive, know that I am with you. Pray and I will listen. It is my will. I answer all prayers even if you don't think I do. Sometimes you are immersed in a lesson. One that you haven't quite gotten. Don't give up. Keep talking to me. Together we will get there. This I know. Be thy will. Thy will be done.

Trust. That is the word for this lesson. I realize it may be hard to think I'm with you as another man points a gun at you. Or as you take a needle and shoot some medicine into your arm. My child in pain. I hear you. All of you. Yes, life can be hard. But it makes the good times that much more enjoyable. If there were always good times, what would be the point? Things would get boring. I hear you already. You are saying you would take the boring. The dullness. The mundane. But where is the growth? Take this as your purpose. For you see it is important to grow. That is the whole point. That is what makes life interesting and a challenge at the same time. The daunting chore. The way to the kingdom. Here my words – Challenge, learn and grow. This is my will. I know some of you don't want to hear this. But this is the truth.

Lesson 17

For this is my will. Words you hear often. Let's talk about their meaning. *"My will"*. What does those divine words truly mean? Do I command you to be a certain way? NO! Do I will you? NO! Do I force you? NO! The answer will always be no! I will never force or demand anything on you. You have the power. What I am asking is for you to listen to my prayer. My desire. My wish. For that is what true love is. It is never forced or demanded upon anyone. Even for me. I do not push. Remember this. Don't go against your free will. Open your heart. Find the love and follow that. Listen. Do what feels right! Be strong. That is what I would do and so should you.

LESSON 18

Archangel Michael comments

Take my will. Do thy will. Be thy will. Put them on your posts. For this I wish for you my sisters and brothers. There is so much to learn. I command you. (he says with a smile). Be strong. Take my words and display them on your posts.

For the weak, the hungry, the poor and the rich. I give you my hand this daily bread. If I could take your pain away I would. Know I am with you listening. I hear your prayers also. Your songs of hope. Your bellows of pain. I wrap my wings around you. Caressing you all the same. Trust we are with you. For the shadows of death are upon you, hallowing your name. Take these words I give you. Hold them to your heart. Beat them to your soul. These words I do declare. "Love" It is that simple. You are loved, loving and loveable. No matter what you have done. We love you so. And so it is. Rest assured this is the way. The path to freedom. It is yours to have. The road may be deep and murky. Filled with rocks and dirt. Keep trenching through. You will get there in your own time. The great kingdom is there for all who desire it. Desire that is the magic word. You must want it with ALL your heart and all your soul. For those who don't dream of it, that is ok too. We still love you. But for those who do, it is there for you. With all the brilliant colors and wonderful smells. When you are ready. And only then will your desire be meant. Don't give up. The time will come in all its grandiose.

LESSON 19

G-D is back

Freedom, what is it? What you consider freedom may be different to your neighbor. It is a relative term. Take what it means to you. Write it down. Picture it every day. As long as it is realistic we will grant you your wish. Even I can't work the impossible. I do what I can according to the laws of the universe. I do my best. For those that feel hopeless or stuck. Think of it as a lesson. Discover what you are learning from it. What you are getting out of it. I realize this simple act can be difficult. Especially when you are so deep in the middle of it. Freedom can be a mindset. A way to view the world. Imagine you darn rose colored glasses. When they are on things are great. You have plenty of money, food and support. You have a place to call home and people around you for love. But as soon as the glasses come off it is all gone. So keep the glasses on. Be that freedom you see. Become it. Feel it. Think about it every minute of the day. Your freedom will be in your gasp. Success is near. But hold on to those rose colored glasses for there will be a next time.

LESSON 20

Lightness vs. Darkness

Is this evil vs good? Not really. Inside us all is both. We are capable of both. Which one comes forward depends on you. What thoughts have you been thinking? What actions have you been doing? How have you been towards your friends, your neighbors and even towards yourself? This is what we call love vibration. The greater your actions are, thus the stronger your love will be. And therefore when you do less that is when the darkness can penetrate. Think of it like this, when you have less love there isn't a wall to fight off the darkness. Almost like a foundation. Or look at it this way, when you go to the gym and build muscle to make you strong or do cardio you are building your heart muscle to keep you healthy. The strength you build with love is the same way. That is the purpose of "being loving" or doing love actions.

When darkness does emerge it takes over. You get mad at your neighbor and it keeps building till you explode and pick up a gun. Walk over and shoot. Now the darkness is so strong, someone else picks up on these vibrations and they do hateful things. This is what being connected can do. So if someone is spinning a negative way it will spread. On the flip side you have the ability to stop that motion and spread love.

Thus watch what you think, say and do. For the sake of society. Lightness vs. darkness is an internal force that spreads like wild fire.

LESSON 21

Being of sound mind and body. We take those words literally. Your minds are very strong. It controls most things. As in previous lessons, it controls the lightness and darkness. It also controls your thoughts which control your health. Take this seriously when I say of <u>sound mind and body</u>. You have the power to be well. It is not entirely up to the medical personal. Since you have me inside and thus are creating on your own. YOU create your world, your life. The mind which is your thoughts, your values, your beliefs. That is how you are you. Dissect those things. Pull them apart. Watch what you do. First of all you are not a victim! You have the power to rise above. It is not your fault that Uncle X hurt you. Or it is not who you are to come from lack of coins. Every one of you has the power to take control of your world. Rise above what has happened and become something great!!! I know this to be true. I have seen some of you do this. However, there are those of you who like to dwell in the "oh me" syndrome. I can't do that, I can't become that. Get that out of your mind. Take those beliefs and wash them away. You are not a victim!! Take control of your life. You have the power. Don't let the past control you! I once saw a young man so abused and beaten down every day of his life. Then one day he woke up and said no more. He left his home as a young boy. Went out on the streets and was able to procure food and shelter. He did this for several years. Finally a friend came upon him. Took him in. Fed him. Taught him right from wrong. And clothed him. He went on to college and created great things. Don't go down the "woe is me" road. Stand up and be strong. Create a good life. Every one of you has the ability. Life is short. Make the most of it.

LESSON 22

The clash between what is right and what is wrong. This is different than light and darkness. Inside of everyone there is the ability to know what you should do. Now somewhere you were taught from an early age the wrong way. I get it. Hopefully somewhere down the road these people will notice a different way. And they will come to believe something new. Others will never change. The things you learn as a child has a way of sticking around. I get it. Hopefully this book will open your eyes. Change your beliefs.

Things I consider wrong:

1. If a boy is a boy, great. But sometimes that boy feels more like a girl. That is ok! There are times we get mixed up and the bodies don't match the mind. Please have compassion! It is wrong to discount these folks. Let them feel and be who they are. They should be able to use the bathroom they relate to.

2. Men can marry women or men. Just as a woman can marry whom she chooses. When someone else decides for them how they should be, that is wrong and judgmental! You know how I feel about judging your neighbors. Marriage isn't for everyone but for those that choose to spend their life with someone, they should be able to do as they wish without others giving them a hard time. It is all about freedom and creating the world of your desire.

3. It upsets me when I see hatred of your neighbors. I have said this before but it is worth repeating. We are all one! I don't care if someone is black or white or yellow or brown. You are all my children. And equal in my eyes! If you bleed is it not all red? If you speak is it not the same. In other wards doesn't everyone want love,

money and friends? Everyone desires the same things. Everyone deserves to be able to acquire it. You are all the same in my eyes. Remember this for it is so. There is no such thing as one race is better than the other. I am tired of seeing the injustice treated to my children. This must stop now!! Put your fellow man on your back. Carry him and he will therefore carry another. The chain will grow tall and strong.

4. Those with excess money should share their wealth. Help those that have little. I'm not saying that if you do have many coins you should feel guilty. No enjoy it but also spread it around.

What I am saying is if you do have the luck of bathing in riches don't flaunt it. Be modest. If you want to drive a Maserati than drive one. For that keeps jobs flowing. Then at the same time keep your house modest. Don't do both grandiose. Don't go overboard on the material items. This will allow more of your money to be free to help others who are not as lucky in this lifetime to have. Don't feel guilty if you have. Enjoy it but just spread it around. Pay someone else's utility bill or buy them some clothes. Remember we are connected. We are all family.

LESSON 23

Trust in G-D - I don't feel everyone does this as much as they should. There are times you question why things are happening. And you don't know what my plan is or cannot see the big picture. Rest assured there is a plan. A "blue print" to my madness. Everything I do, I do for a reason. For example, when the Dodgers play Philly, (I love baseball). The coaches start out with a plan. As the game develops there are twist and turns. Suddenly there are two players out and one on 3rd base. Will the player slide into home and make it safe or will he get forced out. It is up to the other team. It is not up to the player running. It takes team work. Every player working together for one cause. Sometimes it works out and other times it won't. But there was a plan. It has to play out. It may seem cruel or unnatural. It may seem like I'm not rooting for your team. I am. I have to let all my players' tradeoff for the glory of winning. However when you see the big picture everyone is truly a winner. It is not about the final outcome. But about the way it is played. The joy of it. The twists and turns. The outs and the homeruns. When the score is 7-0 and they think there is no hope. That is when I step up and have a plan. It might not be what you want to see for this game. But there is a reason. You might ask – a reason your team is losing? Yes. Everyone has their turn in the lime light. It may not be yours right now but eventually if you practice hard enough, go out every day and practice being the best player you can. I'm not expecting a world of Babe Ruth's. But a universe of Joe Schmoozes. The mediocre guy. He's the one who won't give up. That takes the advice from his coach. The guy who keeps throwing the ball even when his shoulder hurts. The guy that slides into home plate just as the buzzer sounds and wins the game. Now that is trust! Keep looking at the big picture. Hold your head up high. Look at the stars. I am there with you. Even when the chips are down. Trust me I do have a plan.

LESSON 24

Laughter is the best medicine. Laugh! Don't take things to serious. Enjoy the process. A child runs around and laughs in the wind. Then something happens as you become adults. I guess it is the pressure of paying the bills, going to work and taking care of the kids. Stop, smile and be more like that child. Run through the sprinklers. Run naked in the backyard. Be free. The simple act of feeling joy can save your life. Don't worry what others say. Tell them you are doing what G-D said to do (within reason). Don't be silly so often that you get labeled crazy. But once in a while let your "hair down". Go to a comedy house. Laugh so hard your insides are jiggling around. Be that child. Look at life with wonder and amazement. Experience the ecstasy of trying new things. Dip your toes in ice. Breathe in new and exciting smells. Take the time to enjoy the finer things. So when things seem dark and you feel down, take your shoes off and run barefoot in the grass. Do something you would not normally do. Raise your arms in the sky and jump. Don't keep the weight of the world on your shoulders. That is for me to do. It is my job to watch over you. Release the pressure.

LESSON 25

Togetherness

Being of sound mind and body. When you think about it that says a lot. Who is to judge what "sound" is. What one neighbor would call "normal" another might not. When I say it, I'm talking about general population. The average person. Not the exceptional or not one in need of aid. Just the average guy next door. Why should we care about this you say? I bring it up to prepare you for what I say next. Being of sound mind and body is also a legal term. That meaning is not what this is about. Don't misunderstand me. I care deeply about all of you. The average Joe has the responsibility of taking charge with most things. (In most cases). I am aware of the exceptions. The average person is bright and intelligent. He knows how to get things done. You rely on him and hope he or she knows what to do. I also rely on her. He or she is my messenger. My right hand person. Listen to them.

I mention this because I want you to learn from each other. Trust each other. Respect each other. Become one. Multiple brains work better than one. Don't go it alone.

Take for example the baseball team I mentioned earlier. They couldn't play the game alone. Each player needs each and every one. Or the team falls apart.

LESSON 26

The awakening heart

Cold as it may seem. Some of you need to find more love in your heart. The power of love is undeniable. Love can solve many solutions.

First you ask, how do you get there? Start with being of service to someone. Help them mow their lawn or change their light bulbs. Feed the poor, help the unfortunate. Be my right hand person.

Another way to increase your love is to love yourself. This I see is a real problem. The loathing and distrust for yourself has been growing exponentially over time. I believe you are too hard on yourselves. You don't give yourself enough credit for what you do know or are capable of. Wrap your arms around yourself, hold your arms and say "I am ok". I know you can't be perfect but there is so many great things every one of you have already done.

Make a list of all the good you have accomplished so far. Then to balance the negative part, make a list of what you want to work on. Yes even those that have committed a murder or have stolen have the ability to find love in their heart. They might have to dig deeper but I know everyone of can do it.

Once you find that love you will feel like a weight has been lifted. That heaviness is the darkness. Once that is gone the things you can accomplish is endless. So when you hear love heals all, what it really means is that the darkness is gone. Think about it. Do you want to stay in the dark? Open your eyes, look in the mirror and say these words. "You do amazing things like _____" (pick one from your list). Do this twice a day. Everyday.

This would be a great thing if we could increase our self-love. I hope you all understand how important this is. If you have self-love than your ability to have compassion and patience will be greater. The two go together.

LESSON 27

Going back to the sound mind and body. Before we talked about the mind now I mention the body. It is the only vessel you have right now. Take care of it. Work out, drink little and don't smoke tobacco or do drugs! I did not give you life for you to abuse it. I gave you a healthy body it is up to you to keep it that way. Another benefit of exercise is the way it elevates your mood. And thus the saying "being of sound mind and body". Exercise connects it all. Even if it is just a walk around the neighborhood. Get out and move. Do what you can and then keep increasing it. Push yourself to move, make it harder and longer to reap the full benefit. I heard you say "use it or lose it". That is true for the body. Old age won't be as difficult if you take care of the body early on.

Long time ago people had to work hard in their everyday lives. They would hunt for food, build homes, walk a ways for water and then carry it all the way back. Now you sit around watching TV or staring at your computer screens. This needs to change for the better of mankind to advance in the best way possible. Get off the couch. Stand up from your computer. Get moving. Somehow find the time. I know it's hard. Try walking during your lunch break. Get up early or stay after work. It doesn't have to take long. Just do it.

LESSON 28

When people get severely ill, I often hear you ask why this has to happen. I realize there are different varying degrees of sickness. I'm talking about the extreme illnesses. Those with cancer, lymphoma, and migraines. Age has no bearing to this. I'm sorry for the pain it causes. However, it is there to teach a lesson. Sometimes the lesson is for you to appreciate your health. Other times the lesson is for a family member to realize something. I am not cruel. I always have a reason. If this happens to you, stop and look for the lesson. It is there somewhere. Quite your mind and go within. You will figure it out. In your grief or when you are mad for having to deal with an illness, contemplate what you can learn from this.

You might ask about the kids with spina bifida, cliff pallets, autism, or Down syndrome. The list goes on and on. One word, compassion. They are strong souls who never ask "why me?" They take their challenge in stride and never feel like a victim. It is a matter of alchemy. I want every man or woman to see these individuals and give them compassion and not look at them as if they are a monster. These kids have so much love that they enhance the lives around them. Their self-love is tremendous. We can all learn from them. So don't look at them with pity but rather gratitude, for they are showing you that love comes in varying degrees of gratefulness.

LESSON 29

We begin today with the saying "take things in stride". There may be days it seems impossible. Patience, patience my children. Open your hearts. Remember I always have a plan. Even when things seem dismal. And there is no hope. Hang on a little longer. Nothing lasts for long. Things will change. Life is constantly moving, rotating, growing and fading. It may seem like life is forever unpleasant. But just as the tides in the ocean come and go so too will your turbulent time. Hang on. Pray to me. I am there for you. Even in your darkest of time. Stay the course. The storm will be over soon. You are strong and will come through this shinning like the brightest star. I only make strong souls so I know this is so. Not weak ones. And I only give you what you can muster.

If I could take your pain away I would. However it is there for a reason. A plan so big only I can know for sure. Believe me when I say "I've got your back". Don't give up. I can't stress this enough. Stay the course. Don't try to end things. It will pass! For I love you so.

LESSON 30

I hold my children to the highest of standards. Live by my rules:

1. Don't lie, cheat, steal or cuss.
2. Be patient, compassionate and strong
3. Know I love each and every one of you the same
4. Honor your elders. This includes your teachers and your parents
5. Love your family with all your heart. With all your might. They will always be there for you.
6. Never stop reading and learning – open books. It will help strengthen your brain and make life more interesting.
7. Listen to my words. For this I command you. Trust in my work. Trust me. I know what is best.

I know these words may seem simple but believe me, I know it will help in your journey of life.

The next section of this book will be different. It is not a how to live but rather more about what to believe and not to believe. I know some of this information will be new or hard to trust in my words. I implore you to open your hearts and your minds. This information is true.

I start with the story of the beginning of time. That first burst of light. An explosion started life as you know it. Trees emerged. Land began and the tides of oceans rolled in. The land of dinosaurs began. The first creatures I invented. They were my test. An experiment to see how man would behave. Think about it. Some would fight each other while others stayed calm. Some ate only plants while others ate only meat. And others ate everything. Soon I was ready for man. The cave man emerged. He knew nothing. I had to teach him language, fire, how to hunt, just about everything you can imagine.

Then came woman. A companion for man. I didn't want anyone to be lonely. A person that would be different than man. A person that would think differently. A person that would complement man.

Just as there were many different dinosaurs, there were different types of man and woman. Just like in today's world, early man and woman had different desires and wants. Some came together to procreate while others stayed by themselves, not interested in much more than survival.

Time went on. Their ability to advance and emerge developed. There were mistakes made. Yes, I'm not perfect either. I got disappointed in the behavior of my children. At times I wanted to start over. But I soon learned things would not change. There would always be arguments, cheating, stealing and disloyalty. I had to expect this. The darkness can be very strong even for me.

So I let you be. I allowed the prejudice. I allowed man to have slaves. I allowed the conflicts. I allowed the stealing. For I know a greater world would emerge. Now is that time. Things need to change immediately. I know the darkness will still exist but the truth must emerge. I'm tired of all the false stories. You have developed into higher beings. The time for this information to be accepted has come to fruition. The world is changing for the better and so have you.

The wrath of G-D. What does that mean? I understand you think when I get mad the sky opens up and lightening hits the ground. Wrong. That has more to do with the atmospheric pressure. When I get mad chaos happens. People get upset for little to no reason. Cars and planes have difficulty. My children go nuts in the streets. I can hear you now saying – well that happens all the time. Not really. I rarely get mad. You would have to see a lot of those things emerge. Not just a few. This is due to our connectedness. Remember, I said earlier we are one! And what happens to people when they get mad? They do things unconsciously, without being of sound mind and body. Their minds are acting on impulse. Rest assured I hardly ever get that upset.

Getting back to the story of time. Man started becoming more and more sophisticated with each invention. Unfortunately, prejudice and lack of compassion became stronger and stronger. To the point I get mad.

That's when I stepped in and gave you the 10 commandments and released the Jews out of bondage. I had hoped when the Romans experienced the plagues they would have changed and became more compassionate. Unfortunately they did not. They continued with beatings and treating their fellow man horribly and thus people around the world did so too.

(The all connected syndrome at work even then.)

You have the ability to end prejudice. I implore you to stop this madness. I don't want to start the plagues to pour down again, but I will if I need to. Open your hearts!! Love each other for you are all brothers and sisters.

As we move more into the technology area, where we are today, not a lot has changed. Conflict still exists, lack of compassion and beliefs of idols still abound. In some ways you have come far but in others you are still the same my children. We need to work on this. Keep trying. I know some day at least the prejudice will decrease and love will grow stronger.

Religion, the belief of me and the study of our history is important. I want you to understand and respect your past. For that is the only way to move forward. A day at a time. All we have is time.

I know Joshua (commonly known as Jesus) has a lot to do with religion and he is very important to many of you. He is my son just as you are. I sent him to life (the human way) to try to reduce conflicts, prejudice and increase love. It worked. He gave people hope and something to focus on when things get dark. Some of the stories are not true about him however. If you consider bringing more awareness to your life about love, compassion and liberty, then yes he is a savior. That is very important. He has helped me a lot and still does. You can pray to him and he will respond. However, and this is very important, you are ALL my children. All equal in my eyes. I do not forsake one if he does not believe. I don't love one more than another. We will speak more about Joshua later since he is very important to our story.

You are divine. You are perfect and not born with evil or impurities. For I, G-d is wise and Omni important and thus are you. I know I have mentioned my distain with my children but the positive outweighs the negative.

In the beginning man looked out for himself. He didn't care about anything other than survival. He hunted, fished, and slept. Before long more and more men, women and children emerged. Soon colonies came together. Relationships became important. It didn't take long for disagreements to appear. And the groups started to divide. Time went on. Groups got bigger and bigger. Conflicts also grew. The larger the group the larger the conflict. It seems they go hand in hand.

I sent my right hand man to try to calm the conflicts. Joshua (Jesus) did what he could. He taught what I wanted to try to curb the disorder. But to no avail. Things didn't change. My children you are a very stubborn group. Your way is NOT the way! It is time for change. Time to become a people of love and forgiveness. I know you are thinking that you do these things. Yes to a degree but I know things can become even better. I want to see more love! More forgiveness. More compassion. Walk in the shoes of someone you are afraid of. Look around you. Who do you think is inferior to you? Go to his or her home. Have a meal together. Get to know each other. Reduce the conflict. It will always be there but take it into your hearts to improve. Go to the other side. Do as Joshua was doing. Become him. Think to yourself, how would he handle this? The answer will come. Open your hearts. Show the world we can become better. A closer group whom works together as one.

I often wonder if in the beginning I should have forced this love and compassion on you, maybe then things wouldn't be as bad as they are today. I love you all and know what you are capable of. Joshua tried. So can you. Become one. Face your fear. Conflict is based on fear. Fear of your fellow man. They might do things differently. They might look different. But you are all the same!! I can't stress that enough.

Listen to Dori. She is to continue on with Joshua's work. Help her. She is not perfect and needs everyone's aid.

I have mentioned Joshua (Jesus). I want to clear up any confusion. He is my right hand man but so are you. Joshua got it early. He knows how to love all in spite of your differences. Joshua knows my lessons. And yes he is great. I couldn't have done things without him. He has been a huge help. Think of him as a big brother showing you the way.

However, he is not a savor as you would like him to be. And he is not me. He is my son but so are you. Joshua continues to do my work. He is there for you. Call out to him. Pray to him. He will continue to be there for you.

Express amazement in the beauty of things created. Some by man and some by me. I bless all my children. Listen to my words for this is so. Open thy book. Read my words. Hear my song of life. I bless you all. Here O Israel. Open thy hearts, for the heart is the beating drum of what is true.

Joshua ben Joseph (Jesus) now speaks

Hear father's words. Know you are my brothers and sisters. Take his words to heart. Inscribe them on your posts. Teach them to your children. Honor his wisdom.

Long time ago I tried to teach these lessons. Some of you got it while others did not. Hopefully this time more will remember my words. Become the creator within. Beat these words into your being. Fill them with Aba's (father's) words. Now I am going to teach you a few things.

Jesus on Compassion

Kindness matters. Even when the lady at the checkout lane at the grocery store is slow. Or when the car in front of you cuts you off. Don't get mad. Maybe they are having a bad day. Or maybe something just happened or they didn't get enough sleep. Or the person on the other end of the phone didn't get proper training. Have you ever thought that they just didn't know how to read the report? Keep these things in mind next time you get frustrated. Ponder about the possibilities of why people are doing the things they are doing.

I know you are capable of feeling and understanding many great things. So spread your heart and your mind to open further. Don't get mad at your brother or sister. Stop and think first. Think of the possibilities of why events are happening as they do.

Be that person that picks up litter as you walk the dog. Help the elderly person cross the street. Listen to your neighbor's problems. We all need each other. Have you ever felt admired for something you just accomplished? Imagine your neighbor needs the same. Put your feet in their shoes. Feel what it's like to be them even if you don't agree with what they stand for. Understand we all believe different things. Have compassion for their ways even if they are not pure. Be there for them. Even the introvert thrives on friendship. We all need each other in so many ways.

In the book of life we walk down a path of pure bliss. Then one day a boulder falls down and forces us to go a different way. Do you get mad at the boulder? Do you hit it or kick it? NO. You find a way around, do you not? That is life! And you know there will be many boulders – some big, some small. The path you take is not engraved in stone. It is flexible. Think of it as made out of rubber, soft and bendable.

JOSHUA (JESUS) ON HELPING OTHERS

Be of service to someone every day. Part of this blends with the previous lesson. However, it goes further. I want you to reach out to your fellow man, brother or sister. Look for something you can do each and every day. There is so much aid to be given. Don't forget about the environment. Pick up other people's trash. It all belongs to us anyways. Don't let the birds get tangled in it or the frogs to swallow the plastic. Get out there and do your bit.

Yes feeding the poor and the sick is helpful but don't forget the kids. These little souls don't always have money. And their parents don't always share or choose to help their offspring. These kids are lost in the barrage of life. Search them out. The schools do a great part in helping them but more can be done.

As you can see there are many ways to be of service. Some more difficult than others. Find something every day and do it.

Joshua (Jesus) on Open Mindedness

Open your ways. Going back to my boulder story, there are many ways around the rock. One way is not any better than the other. And that is also so for the ability to know what is right or wrong. What path you take may be right for you but understand that it is not always your brothers' choice. Same goes for religion. Be understanding of others beliefs. We will all get back home one way or another. The surroundings along the way just changes. Be understanding. Know there are many ways to arrive at the kingdom of heaven. Don't take pity on them if someone doesn't believe as you. Trust they are doing what is best for them with the knowledge that came from the way they were raised, and thus is affecting their actions. I can't stress this enough. Religious differences are a huge issue. I get it and so must you. Open your mind to hearing about their beliefs. You might learn something interesting. It is not how we get there that matters but what we do along the way.

Joshua (Jesus) on Affirmations

We begin today by talking about the study of the belief of affirmations, which is when you continually repeat words for something great to happen. You must feel the words in your total being. Say the phrase like you know it already happened.

Many great things can happen when you believe. I used this technique often when I was human. For example, it was used when I fed the hungry with 5 loaves of bread and one fish. Now G-D stepped in and helped but the technique can work when you are sick and need to feel better or when you want a certain vehicle or even desire to visit a certain destination. Say the affirmation often – all day in fact. It doesn't matter how you say it. It is like that saying you have "Just do it".

Affirmations can even make you laugh. For example, "I have a brown dog. He is fluffy and small." Simple as this is if repeated enough it could remind you of a poem by a child. And who couldn't smile with that?

The trick is to say them throughout the day and often. Believe you already have what you are looking for. Feel it. The universe will bring you what you want within reason. We can't bring you a million dollars but we can open the doors to a better job, or a close parking spot.

Write down what you want to happen. Burn it on your brain. (Not literally) Become it as it has already happened.

Joshua (Jesus) on Trust In G-D

Be as one with G-D our creator. This means to trust the All Knowing. Know he is with you in your heart and your soul. Together you create. (That is why affirmations work). Trust in him that things will work out.

"Let it be for he knows best. He has a plan. For it is so."

That is one of my favorite sayings. When I was tied up on the cross, I said that over and over. We don't know the big picture. We can only see what's around us. By trusting in the All Mighty we can release our fears, are tension, and are hopes for something better. In other words, surrender. I realize this is a large obstacle in many lives. It is easier to think with our egos and our brains. But put that aside. Think with your heart instead. I know things will change for you if you allow it.

Joshua (Jesus) on Kindness

Be kind to all. I can't stress this enough. The world needs more kindness and patience. I know we have brought this up earlier but it is something worthy of repeating. We would love to see more acts of kindness. It seems the world has become centered around the "me" syndrome. The self-motivated aristocratic self. We have heard you say things like, "I can steal this to get more money." It doesn't matter who gets hurt in the meantime. So you roll over your business partner. Who cares, you got the account. No that attitude must stop. It shouldn't matter who wins the race. Another example we don't like to see is the lack of effort a worker puts into his job. If you don't like the work get something else. Do the best you can in your work. Smile, open the door for your coworker. Be happy you have a job. Treat it as something you are doing for me. Don't skimp on the quality of your effort. Always do your best. I dislike it when I hear lies told just to get the sale. Remember I'm always listening.

Being kind stretches to ALL areas of your life. Personal and professional. Children I have not forgotten you. Yes you too can do with a dose of kindness. I see so many unkind acts from pushing each other down on the playground to cheating on exams, or even lying to your parents. Yes, I see all. Is that what you want me to notice? Be brave, show your true nature. The pure one, I know it can be scary at times. Yes your parents might get mad but honesty is always better. Remember I'm watching over you as well.

The world revolves around *all of* us. We need each other and not to use one other. We also don't want you to think only about yourself. Life is better with team work. A team that *every* player reaches the finish line with the same amount of abundance. All together as an equal.

Joshua (Jesus) on Keeping Life Exciting

When we are small our bodies are limber. And our minds think the world is a scary place. As time passes our bodies grow and mature becoming stiff. We see things differently. We experience things in a new way. Our knowledge of how the world is grows as well. Perhaps when we are young the world is a big wonderful place. Then, as we grow we become jaded and bitter. We become set in our ways, more ridged. The excitement of seeing things with joy and wonder disappear. Life becomes dull and boring. The daily toll of work and paying bills becomes the dance we step to time and time again. During this routine some will experience that childlike joy. While others will dance to a slow and dark song. What makes the difference you ask?

In order to be one of the ones with the upbeat song and dance you must have courage. The desire to try new things. Get out of your routine. I know work is import and I don't want you to do anything that would jeopardize your job. So try doing the little things. Get up an hour earlier and try something new. For example paint, do yoga, walk your dog. Do something different at some different time of the day. Periodically shake things up. Don't let the hum drum of daily life become your dance. Throw a little jazz in with the rock-n-roll. Wear a silly outfit to work one day. It will make the constant rhythm of life become exciting again.

Life can be fun. It is all in the way we perceive it. The way we choose to dance the steps. It is your choice. Do you want life to be a steady beat or do you want to throw in a few crescendos here and there? One of my favorite things to do is play in the rain. Let the cold drops hit your face. Getting outside your comfort zone is another way to put it but don't feel you have to go to any extreme. Like I mentioned earlier something as simple as wearing your clothes differently will work just as well.

How are you going to dance today?

Joshua (Jesus) on Different Ways To Be Powerful

When I was a boy there was this man. He was tall, thin and very strong. He taught me different ways to be strong. One way was to lift heavy things every day. Another way is to think like your fellow man. Get into their head. Know what they are thinking and thus you can figure out ahead of time what to say to get your meaning across. If you know how your friend believes then that makes it easier. For you see when you know someone is going to sway a certain way then you take that knowledge and word your desire around that. For example, if someone feels he or she is round, then I would start out saying round people may believe they eat too much but I feel it is more of a metabolism thing, and then I would state what I wanted them to trust me with.

Another way to be strong is to think smart. What I mean by this is if you feel smart you are. When you believe this many powerful things can happen. So you see not only can your muscles grow big and powerful but so can your attitude and knowledge of the way others think which is also quite strong and enduring. Be wise and powerful.

Joshua (Jesus) on Standing Up To Your Beliefs

My human father once said to always stand tall. What he meant by this is to stand up for what you believe. Don't slump and look down or look away. If there is something to be said, stand straight, raise your head and speak out. So that is what I did. I stood in front of people with my head held high or sometimes looked them in the eye and spoke my words. I announced my values, my beliefs. I didn't care what others would think. I took my words and with all my conviction belted them out.

I tell you this story to get my desire for you to stand your ground when you believe a certain way. Don't teeter this way and that. Yes it is wise to listen to others beliefs. And do your research on why you think the way you do. But once you are completely clear then be strong. Stand on your own two feet. However, be kind about it. Don't shout or cuss at them. Speak calmly and quietly. It is important to not let people roll over you. Remember, I know you are smart and have things worthy to express.

The heavenly father has mentioned this but I too want to talk about kindness. It is important to talk about again and again. For we see so little of this. Slow down. Don't hurry through life. Take time to smell the flowers. If you are so busy running to work, taking care of the bills, and the house, the stress will build. Slow down. Take a minute to just stop, blow the air out and breath. When you relax it will be easier to be kind. It is like a rubber band being twisted around a poll. Around and around it goes till nothing is left. Then suddenly the rubber band snaps!. Just imagine if while it was wrapping around the poll and occasionally it untwisted a lap or two. The end would take much longer. And the rubber band would be loser, not so tight.

My friends slow down!! Take a breath. I know you can do it.

Joshua (Jesus) on Life Is a Mirror

Once when I was a boy a man taught me to stand tall and believe in mankind. We are all good. Don't believe in the worst. Think positive. Humans can be kind and considerate. If that is truly what you feel then that is the type of person you will reflect in your life. Think of life as a mirror. How you feel inside is what you will draw to you or reflect back. If you think most people are dishonest then that will be what you bring into your life.

Close your eyes. Take a few deep breaths and blow them out one at a time. Think about it. What do you feel most people are? Are they kind? Are they liars? Are people out to get you?

If it is something negative change that. Change your thoughts. Our thoughts control what kind of life we will have. Ideas we hold in our heads are so important. They can even control how healthy we are. If you have a lot of negative or even disappointing thoughts, those turn into dis-ease.

G-d and I want you to have a happy, joyous life. But when we see hurt, deceit, or despair we think you would prefer that. And thus that is what you will receive. Do some soul searching. Write down how you *truly* feel. Do you feel people are basically good? If not figure out why. How did those thoughts start? Do you feel lonely or lack thereof? Change that thought and feel abundant. Notice I said *feel*. Don't just think it. It is important to really believe and feel inside to your very core that life is abundant and has everything you desire. A life full of kind people and wealth.

I can hear you now. I can hear your wheels grinding. I'm not saying everyone will become billionaires. Abundant or wealthy are terms that are relevant in perspective and different to everyone. We all need different things at different times. We can all be wealthy in our own ways.

This brings up a point. Money. Is it the root of all evil? No. Can it cause corruption? Yes. Be careful if you are around people who will do **anything** to get ahead. Believe me I know what it can do. However, if you are so lucky as to be centered on flowing coins. By all means enjoy. Don't feel guilty, but do share it. Allow those gold coins to spread and help others. If you feel abundant with your money you will always have enough. Don't worry it will run out. The more you give, the more you will have. However, at the same time don't hand over your life savings, thinking we will replace it. Sometimes we will but sometimes we won't. So be smart. Take care of your own needs but give what you feel comfortable with.

Joshua (Jesus) on Turning Negative Situations To Positive Ones

How to be wise you ask? That comes with practice. Every time you run into the wall and come through with flying colors, the wiser you become. I'm talking about lessons you have learned well. Every time you are faced with an obstacle, think to yourself, "This will make me stronger". If for some reason you hit the wall and crash and burn, maybe you didn't get the lesson we were trying to teach. Watch out because the lesson will appear again and again till you get it right. Don't despair however. We will only give you what you can handle. If you feel drowning in life's troubles, know we only give you what you can deal with.

Remember, think to yourself how wise is this problem making me. So when a co-worker does something offensive and your situation at home is bad. Breathe, know you are becoming a great master. Plus, think to yourself what this negative situation is trying to teach. Detach yourself from it. Look at it from above. In the heat of an argument step back. Figure out how to learn from it. Sometimes it may take a few days to sink in but rest assured there is always a reason it occurred. Open your mind. The more you get the lesson and know why it is happening the better off you will be. Don't go through life with blind folds on.

Joshua (Jesus) on Fear

In the beginning of my teachings I use to speak about kindness and obscenities. Then I realized it was more about love and forgiveness. Now I truly believe more can be accomplished with understanding people's fear.

You either have fear or you have love. Those with love in their hearts know my lessons. It is those who fear that need my work. These individuals should ask themselves what they are so fearful of. When people get angry it is out of fear. When someone pushes you out of line it is out of fear. When someone holds a gun to your head it is out of fear. When someone cheats on an exam it is out of fear. When someone bullies another it is out of fear. When someone lies to win a bid or get a sale it is out of fear.

Fear is the root of all discord! So when things get tough or difficult stop take a breath and ask yourself where the fear is. I can't stress this enough. If you get nothing else out of these lessons remember this one for it is the most important one.

Don't get me wrong, I want you to learn them all but know I care most about this one.

Joshua (Jesus) on Winning The Right Way

When I was boy out playing ball. We use to fight over who got the ball or even who won. Things don't change much as we become adults. We still fight over who is right or who will get the deal (bid). I'm not telling you not to get that ball. Yes, go after that touchdown. Become a winner. Just do it with grace. Be humble, calm and listen. Open your ears. Listen to your fellow players. Watch for that opening so you can pass the ball to the other player. It is not about who won the game. Although I know most of you feel it is, since you are most affected by the prize. The game is more about getting the ball down the line. Be a strong player. Go ahead be aggressive to a degree. Just play by the rules. Don't cheat or push the other down. Win the game the right way. Open your heart and be kind.

Joshua (Jesus) on Communication

Strength what is it? I talked about it earlier. And now again. It seems a trait most strive for. But what is it really. Are you strong if you can hold up to a hurricane wind storm? Are you strong if you can lift a house? Or how about the strength of an ox plowing a field. That is not the strength I'm talking about. I'm concerned with the strength of the mind. The power of your voice. How do you express your words? This is most powerful. It is like that saying, "Sticks and stones can break my heart but words can never hurt me." Our voices are most powerful. We can change the world by words and that is powerful and strong. When your child comes to you with a question. Don't tell them to go away or belittle them in anyway. Tell your children they are smart, beautiful and strong. Take time to listen to them. Put down your whisky. Look them in the eyes and just listen. They have wonderful things to say. You might learn something from them.

Listen to a person waiting on you at a restaurant. Ask them questions about their life. It is these simple things that can affect the world we live in. Be strong. Be courageous. Be a good listener and that means you need to also ask questions. Part of listening is getting people to talk about themselves.

Who are you going to talk to today? Look around you. Find out who is sitting next to you on the plane, bus or who lives next to you. Be strong. Open your mouth. But only let kind, positive words out. Find the story of those around you. Show you care.

Joshua (Jesus) on Knowing Your Own Values

I have another story when I was a boy. My neighbor came to me one day and asked about my hair. It is curly and dark. He wanted to know if I would ever grow it long. I mentioned it was up to my mom because I didn't care. It was the trend back then for the boys to grow their hair very long. My neighbor didn't like my answer. He pushed me around to be "a man" and decide for myself. From that moment on I stood my ground and decided my own fate.

That is what I want you to do. Do your own soul searching. Figure out what **you** want. Don't do as your neighbor is doing, or the man on the stage or the woman on TV. Reach inside your soul. Ask what you want. Your soul will tell you if you listen. In order to hear, close your eyes, take a few deep breaths, you will either hear or feel what is right. If something doesn't feel good don't do it.

For too long now we have relied on other people's opinion of their values and beliefs. G-D is inside you. I promise you this. Listen to him! He will guide you if you listen. We care. This is the way to his heart. Be strong. Do listen to other people's opinions but figure out what is best for **you**.

Joshua (Jesus) on Opening Your Heart

Take my words and hold them tight. Look at the sky. Notice how blue it is. Look at the green grass. For those who can't see, notice the smells. Look at your surroundings. Be aware of all the wonderful things G-D has created for you. Don't go through life just thinking about yourself. Become aware. Listen to the cars going by. Hear the birds singing. Notice the light poll. Think about how it is made. Who put it up? How did it get here? How about the road you drive on. Who invented the asphalt and think how that has made your life easier. Notice all the things around you that has allowed your life to be more relaxed. Look at the shape of things. What sound does it make? Is it shiny or dull? I think you get what I want you see or hear. Open your mind. See around you. This exercise will open your heart. It will allow you to appreciate G-D and all his wonders. When you do this your vibration will increase which allows your love to grow. You know the answer to life is love. The way to happiness is love. Fill your jar with love. Think of it as a balloon blown up but this one will never pop.

Joshua (Jesus) on Hate

Now that you have a big heart it is time to learn about hate. Not my favorite topic but it must be addressed. We are all born with and experience it. Some more than others. When those feelings come up in you don't squash them down. Recognize you feel this way. Accept it but figure out why. Is it something you fear? Think about that. Often hate stems from fear. What are you so scared of? When someone makes you mad is it because they don't value what you do? Or perhaps it is something they did to you? I get it. Not everyone will see things as you do. Sometimes they will physically hurt you. But know it is coming from fear. Maybe they like to control and they lost that trait with you. Or if the hate is inside of you, what are you so fearful of? Take the time to think about it. Do some soul searching. Figure it out.

The emotion of hate will always be nearby. We are human it is a part of us. Just think of it as a warning light going off. There is a reason for the blinking lights. Would you go through the intersection without caring the yellow lights are going off? Then why would you go through life without listening to your hate. There is always a reason. Deal with your hate and anger. Understand it in your mind. Is it more a dis-like?

Joshua (Jesus) on Forgiveness

It is time to open your mind to new ideas and thoughts and actions. We come to a place where we all need to expand our awareness. Be open to new and exciting possibilities. Here is a thought that most of you have not had before. The idea of becoming victim less. An idea of taking responsibility for yourself. It isn't your fault that Uncle Joe hurt you as a child. It isn't your fault you had to leave work early to pick up a sick child. But you say I have a responsibility to do the right thing. Yes and no. You have the ability to decide how to live. If my child was sick I would pick him up or if I couldn't leave for some reason I would find someone else to pick my child up.

My point being we all have choices. Take control of what you decide and be happy. Don't get mad at your child for being sick. And understand that the person that hurt you has mental issues. It wasn't your fault. The difference between hate and anger is the ability to rationalize the other person's actions. When you are angry or are mad at someone you can't see straight. The emotion takes over. However, hate is just as intense but you are capable of understanding the root cause of your emotion. Either one of these emotions requires forgiveness. After all is said and done, blow out your love. Walk away and consciously forgive the other person. If you don't it will only fester inside. That pain could make you sick. Is that neighbor worth giving you a dis-ease? No. So blow it out and move on. It wasn't your fault!! You did not cause them to be how they are!

Joshua (Jesus) on Taking Pride In All That You Do

The slogan "Make America Great Again" brings up a thought. The American workers. You who are employed and working hard. Take my hand. I'm with you in the fields, the factory plants, and the office buildings. You are creating things first as G-D does. This is important to think about. Take pride in what you do. Be like G-D and do the best you can. Don't slide through half fast. We see so many do this. It is not a wise thing. Be conscientious. I know mistakes will happen, after all that is what being human is. However, it is those of you who do things on purpose that bothers me. Don't rush through your job. Take pride in what you do or find something else.

How you choose to live is very important. Are you going to blame Uncle X for messing up your life? Or Aunt O for introducing you to that drug. NO!!! Take control and forgive. Move on. I know it is hard but being a victim will not open you up to finding all the love you can in order to have a truly happy life. That is the goal after all.

Not being a victim is a tremendous problem for most of you. That is why you will hear me repeat this over and over again. FORGIVE and move on.

Even as simple as driving two hours to work every day with hate and contempt for your job will eat you up. Don't resent your boss. This is not a reason to feel a victim. It doesn't have to be that way. Change jobs or feel validated that you love every minute of the drive. Make it pleasant somehow. Get an audio book, learn a new language.

My point being we all have choices to make on how we are going to react to life. Do the thing that will make you most happy. Own up to it.

Don't go through life with a 50lb. brick on your back. Drop the weight and stand tall.

It all comes down to forgiveness. Know that Uncle X and Aunt O will face their own consequence of what they did to you. It is not up to you. They will have to deal with it. Don't let them control your life. You have a new beginning to carry G-D's love inside. Hold that dear to you. Take some time to look deep inside. Life can be wonderful. How will you choose to live? Full of love or full of disappear? It is up to you. You have the control.

Joshua (Jesus) on Choices

There comes a time in everyone's life to choose a different path. I want each and every one to understand that you choose who you want to live with. How many kids to have. How to earn a living. Life is full of choices. The best thing is you can change. Nothing is written in stone. Life is constantly changing. Just when things are going great something will happen. We do this to make sure you are awake. Or when life keeps throwing you pits. Rest assured eventually you will get the cherry. I love the saying, "If life is a bowl of cherries, why do I keep getting the pits?" One thing is for sure, there will always be change. Just when you think things can't get worse it does. Hold on. The tide will come in and wash it all away. There will be a new beginning. Trust me on this. Don't give up. Just hold on to your boat. Ride the storm out because the sun will come up just around the corner. This I know for sure. Say to yourself:

"Let it be. For it is G-Ds will. He knows best. For this is so."

When I was tied up on the cross, I repeated that over and over. It got me through that time and it will help you out also.

JOSHUA (JESUS) ON BEING MESSIAH

My arch enemy once taught me to be strong. He asked me one day how can I be the messiah. I never said I was. In fact I am not. I am close to G-D but that is all. We are all the same. All children of the All Knowing, the All Mighty. As a child of the All Knowing I tell you from the bottom of my heart he loves us all the same. I was able to hear his words and thus wanted everyone to also know what he desired. We all have different gifts, that happened to be mine. I could have ignored them and become a carpenter like my dad but I choose to spread the All Mighty's words. I didn't get far as a human but in the afterlife my work continues. I have never stopped spreading the All Knowing's teachings. Thus this book, as well as other ones before emerged. I also hear your prayers rest assured. We answer depending on the lesson you need to learn at the time. Just as G-D is listening – so am I.

Do hear my words. I am not the messiah. Just someone with an extra link to G-D. We all have a connection with him. Mine is just a bit stronger. Don't give up on me. I implore you to stay strong and believe in me. I am with you just in a different way.

Joshua (Jesus) on Loving Our Neighbors

Boys will be boys. Just as girls will be girls. We have special traits and abilities. Some get mixed up in the womb. And that is ok. It doesn't matter. We all, no matter what our identity is, open the doors to unique ways to carry our lives. We take these journeys differently. It doesn't matter if we are a woman or man or creative ones in between. We all come from the same source. Thus are all equal in the lord's eyes. So honor your neighbor as G-D commands. Open your hearts and your minds. It is time for change.

Joshua (Jesus) on Sin

Do you aspire to be like me? Then slow down. Take in the air. Breathe with a conscious. Become aware of what is around you. Do my work by looking inside. Open your hearts to those around you. It is not hard. I see some of you talking a big talk. Acting like you have it and do it all the time. But the fact remains. You don't. I see callous indifferences like never before. I witness dishonesty more than ever. For those that do walk the line. I applaud you. I know it is not easy. However, for those who do not, it is time to change your ways. We are watching every one of you. We see what you do. I guarantee you don't want to know our comments. Or feel our disappointment. You think no one knows. But that is false. We always know. If you need help reach out. There are many who can help. Or open a book. There is a lot of great information out there.

We all go to the great kingdom of heaven. However, it is not the same for all. I would love it to be though. So prove me wrong and show me you can change. It may take some work, but I know you can do it. I have seen the cruelest of man wake up to see the light. He became the kindest soul. I know it is possible. You can do it too.

We all sin at times. That is part of being human. It is the one that does it over and over. Those individuals are whom I'm talking about. When we sin, bells go off in heaven. It is not a pleasant sound. We see all and hear everything. Wouldn't it be great to see more compassion and honesty? It is not about what you feel you deserve, or what society owes you. We all go through bad times. It is how we emerge that counts. Instead of thinking you deserve this or that, how about knowing instead you gained a great lesson. And thus you became a better person and learned things no one else can appreciate. Those are gifts so unattainable by most that you should feel special. It is all in the way you see things. The perspective you choose.

We will talk more about that later. For the time being in order to change your beliefs you have to change what you value. And how you feel the universe has treated you.

Take a moment to realize what you really deserve. Be honest. Does it lead you down a good path? Or is it taking you somewhere dark. We all deserve to have the good things in life, but how you get them is what counts.

Arch Angel Gabriel on Getting Through the Difficult Times

There are times when you need to trust that everything will work out for the best. However, there are times when situations seem bleak. Times like now; when war seems imminent, and bombs are lurking in the wings. You say how can this work out for the best? Truth of the matter, it probably won't this time. Some things are out of G-Ds control. The darkness takes over. I wish it wasn't so, but unfortunately it has to happen. The wheels have already been set into place.

I mention world problems because sometimes our own lives can seem bleak but in the long term things will be ok if you learn the lesson that needs to be in place. I have never met an older person who didn't look back at their lives and didn't appreciate the hard times. The trick is to get through it without spiraling down out of control.

When things seem dark, I want to wrap my wings around you and I do at times anyways. If you ever notice a small cool breeze when times are rough, rest assured I am holding you.

I play the role of healer and protector. I use these powers where they are most needed. Call out to me and I will come. I see you as my brother and sister who is in need of my services. When darkness is so thick, I open the light. I am most noticed as human form. When you see a kind stranger emerging from the dust it is me. I get inside your heads to force kindness. Once one person starts it is like a domino, more emerges. It just takes one kind person to start the reaction.

I tell you this because sometimes I need your help to step in and get things started. You will be surprised who else will step up. We have been noticing more and more situations that citizens have come forward with their kindness, but would love to see more. When you are helping, look into the eyes of those most in need. That is when I stretch my wings and wrap them around.

Times can get tough, but know that you are never alone. My biggest advice to you is to reach out your arms and hold them up to the sky, take a breath and then wrap them around you. Imagine my out stretched wings going around you.

Arch Angel Michael on Making Great Things Happen

My biggest responsibility is to bring riches to you. There are many different kinds. For instance when a child comes into the world, that is filled with wealth. Or when you win an award. Or when you fly off a cliff and your shoot opens at just the right time. Fortunes can emerge in many forms. All these things and many others are my work.

Don't curse me when things don't work out as planned. You signed up for it. I'm just there to guide you. To help you float as gently as possible. When things are tight, hold me in your mind. See me giving you what you want. Make it real, feel it, taste it. Call my name. I command you this day.

I know many would like more money, more gold coins. I hear this a lot. Imagine you already have it. See me give it to you. But you still have to do the work. I can't cast a spell and poof it materializes. It doesn't work that way. Go to school or find a mentor. Figure out what you need to do and take action. Then relax and let me take over. Plus, use your mind to imagine me giving you things. It is like the saying, "it takes a village to raise a child". I'm here for you. Every one of you can achieve great things. You just need to believe. When you have faith in yourself, my job is much easier. Take the pressure off yourself. You're not alone.

Arch Angel Michael on Anger

In order to protect and serve we need your help by opening the door to your own kingdom. In order to manifest the beauty inside, put down your guns, and swallow your nasty words. We can only do so much. As G-D told you earlier, we are all creating as one. You have to do your part. We all get angry at times but talking it out works so much better then fighting or using guns. If you have too much fury, walk away.

When tension rises express your concerns and move on.

Arch Angel Raphael on Stress

There is so much beauty in the world. However, with all the stress we don't take the time to stop and see the green grass or the magnificent mountains. To help you relax, take just five minutes a day to breathe or go outside and smell the air. This alone will reduce your stress. The pressures of life will kill you. Find a way to slow down for five minutes a day. I promise you will feel better. And if you can go outside for this rest so much the better.

Stress the most dreaded six letter word. To become conscious of its presence is a beginning to alleviate it. Most people walk around doing their daily tasks without even being aware. Once you acknowledge its presence, do my five minute exercise or bend down to touch your toes and then stretch. These simple things will do wonders for your soul.

Arch Angel Ezekiel
on Gratitude

To have the love of G-D flow through your veins you must first take the action of trust. Trust in the open space of your mind. Fill that space with knowledge. The more you learn, the more your heart opens. Look at art and admire it for its beauty. Read a book and get different perspectives. See a movie and notice the visual essence.

My people, love is all around. Happiness of your soul depends on it. To become the source as one. Show yourself the beauty of the world. Expose yourself. Look around with gratitude. Pull out five things you are grateful for every day. Do it several times a day. Learn to appreciate what we have accomplished for you. There are so many things to admire and that is how to show your love. The more you realize what we have provided for you – the more you will have. If you are always looking at what you don't have the less you will have. It is that simple. You can look at it like this, you are telling the universe you want less when you complain about what you don't have. For example, it doesn't hear you saying you hate your house. The universe believes you want a small house. Another example is "I don't have a good job". When you drop the word don't you are saying you have a good job. Therefore go with gratitude of what you do have and things will expand exponentially. The universe doesn't like to hear you complain. When you show your gratitude at what we have given you we reward your thinking. Those that complain are annoying to listen to. It is like a squeaky voice. It is not pleasant. Think of it as being around a negative or downer all the time. No one likes that. You prefer to be around upbeat happy people. Well, so do we. Gratitude is your reward.

Walk in peace.

Arch Angel Shmuel on Becoming Flexible

My advice to you is to become as one. In order to create the world you long for go back to the beginning of time. When the trees were planted we discovered they had many purposes. They provided shade, support for shelter, nourishment and when climbed, provided a space to hide from predators. We shook those trees and they always bent back into shape. We were amazed with their abilities. Move forward in time to the present. People are like trees. You can accomplish many things. We are just in awe Look at the tree, does it not bend to only bounce back? Few will snap because they didn't know how to be flexible or they fought the pressure of the wind. Don't give up on hope and desire. If one branch of the tree doesn't work out try another and another. The tree will keep growing no matter what happens. A branch might break off but the main part of the tree still exists. Find that part that will work for you and hold on tight. That is becoming as one. Blessings.

Arch Angel Raphael
on Perception

I want to take you to the future. The possibilities are endless. Flying cars, dogs on treadmills and parks in the sky. Things will seem different but in fact they are the same. On the outside it looks different but at the core it is the same. Society still worries about money, how to live in a harmonious world, what kind of house to have, how the children will be safe and what job will make them happy. The basics we experience today will be there tomorrow. Things stay the same for the most part. What will change is how life is perceived. Perception is everything. One person might see the dog walker treadmill as a disaster for the lack of socializing with neighbors. While someone else will sit on the couch while their dog is on the treadmill and love it. It depends on the angle you experience it. If one view doesn't work change it. If your wife beats you, say well she loves me and she is just having a bad day. Or you could leave her to find a woman who doesn't react to a bad day that way.

Perception has to do with what you value. Your beliefs. Look inside what core values are you going to abide with. How one person views things will be different for someone else because their values are different. Take the word perception and break it down. Per – meaning through, ception – to take or accept according to the Latin root word cept. So through what you accept or allow as defined by perception.

This word perception is important because it affects how an event will be handled. Do you treat your neighbor with love or do you say nasty words. What and how you hear them depends on your core values. The next time someone rubs you the wrong way think to yourself about your values. Are you understanding them with love and compassion? And if not why? Where is it coming from? Be conscious of your perception. It is important. In fact make a list of your core values. The more you know about yourself the better.

ARCH ANGEL RAPHAEL
ON LAUGHTER

I have many things to say. When I break bread with my neighbors we enjoy great conversation. We discuss what we have been doing or experiencing. Laughter always ensues. I love to laugh. There isn't anything so terrible that doesn't deserve some kind of humor. Too many times the seriousness of a situation can drag us down. And yes there are times if you started laughing at say a passing in the family you would seem crazy. I'm not talking about those kind of experiences. But rather about more day to day events that seem mundane. Jesus has mentioned to be more "childlike" and I agree. Have more fun and laughter. Don't be so serious. Do silly things. Put a spoon on your nose if you need something to break the ice. It's ok to not be civil all the time. Laughter is a great medicine. A giggle in the stomach can shake things up which can develop into miraculous things.

ARCH ANGEL RAPHAEL ON DARKNESS

Unfortunately, the opposite of laughter is darkness. We all experience it from time to time. It is part of life. It can engulf us like a blanket. Although the darkness can make the good times better. But when you are going through it, it is hard to imagine anything else. You may think we abandoned you. I want you to know that is the furthest thing from the truth. We are always with you! Cry out and we listen. Hold yourself tight for it is us doing the work. I know this may seem strange but darkness can be a friend. We can learn so many things from it. For it is a great teacher. When you are having an unpleasant time, think to yourself, "What am I learning from this. Can it help me go further with my lessons?" Just like you broaden your education in school so do you expand your knowledge of life. I can hear you saying "I would rather not have these times". I get it. But challenges will always be around. So embrace it. Learn from it or the unfortunate situation will either reemerge or it won't leave at all. Take that deep breath in that G-D mentioned and blow out the love. Things won't change overnight. Give it time. Know things NEVER stay the same.

ARCH ANGEL GABRIEL
ON PERCEPTION

I also want to speak on perception. It really does depend on how you view things. It is like the saying about the glass of water. Is it half full or half empty? Take the perception of half full. Is that more positive? Depends on what you need. Are you thirsty or satisfied? Is the glass dirty or clean? Is it small or large? You see many variables go into the equation. Sometimes one way works while another time something else is needed.

Look at it this way. Situations are always neutral. You are the one creating it to be a certain way. If you get mad at a bank teller and are all worked up, first you need to blow out some love, then stop and wonder if the teller received enough sleep the night before, or maybe their child is very sick. Point is you don't know what all the facts are so change your perception. Get back to neutral. Get back to being calm. Try to see the total picture. Close your eyes and try to get in the other person's head. Sometimes you can pick up on what possibly could have happened and why. Trust what you might feel. If you stay mad at the teller, you could be so worked up that you are not in your right mind and you get into an accident. What would that benefit? You now have more problems to deal with. Open your mind to seeing the total picture, the other person's side. Since we are all connected, look through their eyes. Remember you have G-D within. Open that door. The goal is to get back to neutral. Be as one.

Arch Angel Gabriel on Getting Through the Tough Times

In order to take "the high road" you must begin with the low road. Have you ever needed food or shelter or even money? Have you struggled to survive? Cherish those times. They are great moments to master. Notice how you are responding to people and then realize how others look at you. I know it would be best not to have to experience it. Wouldn't it be great if everyone had plenty to eat? Or others had all the gold coins they desired. Life isn't that way unfortunately. Learn from it. Make those times a treasure of education so when it has passed, and it will, you can emerge grander, wiser and stronger.

I hear you saying, "How can I learn when my child is so weak from lack of food?" You gain by realizing your strength is to stay alive. You learn to be resourceful. It is possible in a previous life you had so much food you wasted it and this life you needed to learn how special it is.

When you focus on what you don't have then the universe will continue to give you that. Focus on what you do have. Perhaps you have plenty of water or rice? Be grateful for what you do have. Tell yourself your belly is full. Feel it full. I promise more food will come.

Arch Angel Gabriel on Acquiring All Your Desires

I touched on affirmations in the last lesson. These words are there for encouragement and a way to "reprogram" your thoughts. They are also ways to tell the universe you are in charge and need things to be different. However, you accept what gifts the universe has given you.

Start by writing what you want down. For example, "I have plenty of food. My belly is so full I have to loosen my pants." It is not enough to just say these words. You have to FEEL them. Smell them. Visualize them. See it already happening. You also must repeat it throughout the day. It is not enough to say it a few times. It must be done all day. You do it so much that you become the thought. Say you are working on having more money. How are you going to get it? Is it with a new job or by getting a big contract? Write out exactly how this will be achieved. Then visualize you already having it. You are doing this new job. You are feeling what it is like to do that work. Now repeat this process all day.

1. Write it down
2. Visualize you already have it
3. Feel it
4. Repeat, repeat, repeat

Possible reasons it doesn't work.

1. You are trying too hard without putting in all the steps. You just say the words but have no feeling
2. You must feel AND believe it has already happened.

3. Be careful how you say the words. The universe doesn't hear negative words. Words such as "Don't, must have, need, more of, These are just a few examples. If you are not receiving what you want try rewording the affirmation.

4. Think about where you are coming from. In other words, what is your motive? Is it pure? Are you coming from a place of love? Is your motivation for the higher good? Are you doing this to manipulate someone in order to get what you want? If so it won't work.

5. Occasionally affirmations won't work if you need to learn a lesson. There are times the universe will hold back because it is not of your higher good at that time. But don't give up. Try it again later. They do work. Trust me.

ARCH ANGEL GABRIEL
ON FORGIVENESS

My lesson on forgiveness. I know you have been taught this before but it is one of the largest reasons for difficulties in life. If there are disappointments or lack thereof, you probably need to do some soul searching. Are you being harsh on yourself? We forget to forgive ourselves. We can be our worse enemy. That constant battle inside. We are not thin enough, smart enough, tall enough, rich enough or patient enough, to name a few.

Or perhaps you don't appreciate what you do have, focusing more on the lack there of. The deal you lost, your house isn't as large as your neighbors, your auto isn't as nice, or your need for more clothes. STOP the madness. Be content with what you have. Look around, think to yourself you have what you need. You are blessed with plenty. You will get the next deal. This one wasn't meant to be.

Another thing we beat ourselves up with is our words. We say something to someone that we regret. Or don't say what we should. Either way the "I should have ----, or I could have ---" STOP Forgive yourself! It wasn't meant to be expressed the way it happened. Learn from it. Be aware but then move on. These thoughts can create dis-ease. Be honest with yourself. Accept the thoughts. They are important. Recognize them. Write them down and then throw away the paper. It no longer exists. Fill that space with love instead.

Now we come to the forgiveness of another individual. The person that did something harmful to you, either physically or emotionally. Yes, they had no right to do it. The fact remains they did the act. Maybe it needed to happen because we needed to push you in a direction. We needed to teach you a lesson of forgiveness, or sometimes it happened because of a past karma. You did something to them once before in a different life time and thus their actions were a sense of evening the score card. The universe is complicated. There are many wheels turning. The challenge is to figure out why it happened. Yes it sucks. But in order to increase your capacity for love, you must forgive. If not dis-ease moves in which we don't want. Madness can overtake you. Mentally I like to visualize a dinner party with the person that did me harm. I imagine myself talking to them, telling them how they hurt me. Then I wrap my arms around them and tell them I forgive. All the while I fill up with love. After that it is important to blow out the negative energy. Push it away. Send it on out.

This exercise will help clear the air. One thing for sure is you don't want that extra baggage. There needs to be more space for love. I know it can be hard to forgive. People can be very cruel. I get it. But thank them – mentally and move on. Your best life requires this. Do you want to walk in the shoes of G-D? The All Mighty would forgive. So must you.

What happened to you was wrong, but that allowed you to become a new you – a more compassionate one. Don't let what happened make you sick because if you don't forgive that is what will happen. Show them you are better. I know it is unfair and hard but you have to do it.

Arch Angel Gabriel on Appreciating the Small Things

Take your mind to a new level. Go beyond the daily stress of life. Become a new you. Open the door to love like you have never experienced before. Look around you and smile. Look with wonder at how things are made. The wooden sculpture on your mantel, look how miraculous to have someone carve it like that (even if it was a machine). Or notice your TV, think about all the hours of creation that went into that. Look at the couch you are sitting on, think about the fabric and the cushions someone designed. Thank them for all their hard work. Be grateful for all your belongings, and all the creations that surround you. Notice the little things. Look at the world with wonder and awe. Think about the shoes you are wearing. Wiggle your toes. Be grateful for the leather on the souls and the leather or fabric that encircles your feet. Be grateful for the people who invented the wheelchair. In other wards don't take things for granted. Modern man has come a long way since the days of the caveman. Enjoy it. Respect it. Be as one. Notice the sky, the birds, the mountains and the rain. Just to name a few.

The reason this is so important is because <u>everything</u> has an impact on you. Even the objects we don't even think about. Just because you are not aware of them doesn't mean they don't affect you. When G-D says we are one the All Mighty really means it.

Arch Angel Uriel
on Contempt

I gather you here today to discuss contempt. The definition is when a person doesn't agree with what is going on and thinks the other is not worthy of him or her. In the shadows of dusk or in the morning sunrays their true colors come out. Contempt is not a pretty thing. Just because someone else's ideas are not the same or the color of their skin is not as you would prefer, that is no reason to not have compassion or understanding. There are differences between contempt and bigotry. The latter is a complete misunderstanding or even fear of another. While contempt is knowing deep down something is wrong but still behaves in an unflattering way.

The best way to get over contempt is knowledge. Understand where someone is coming from. Open your mind to new ideas. You might not agree and that is OK. This is what makes the world so interesting. We all have different ways of doing things. The process becomes a swirl of energetic ideas all mashed into one. Once we become one there is no room for contempt.

Arch Angel Uriel on Bigotry

I touched on bigotry earlier and I would like to expand on this. I believe it starts in the home, when one parent thinks they are superior to another. We can break it down further and it becomes fear. If there is no love then there is fear. A false sense of fear that an individual will harm you in some way. A fear the other will become better then you or a fear they will find out you are not as great as you seem. The constant talk of telling a child someone else is dirty or dumb or worse yet a criminal. This gets into the minds of children and they react. It becomes so engrained they know nothing else. It becomes meshed into their souls.

I guarantee we are ALL the same! ALL created equal from the hand of G-D. This includes women and men. We came from one source with one purpose, to get to the kingdom of love and understanding. If I can change the path of one child to stand up to their parents beliefs, I would be happy. Enjoy a meal with someone you dislike. There is something to breaking bread with people that opens the door to understanding.

JOSHUA (JESUS)

As we close this part of the book I hope you understand all we really want is for there to be more kindness and compassion in the world. From our view point it is lacking something awful. We hope you will take this practical guide and open your hearts. Learn to treat ALL as equals. Have patience when anger abides. Be of service to those in need. Open your pocket book when needed. Be modest in nature and most of all love one another.

Blessings to all. Know we love every one of you. Life is a journey. There are ups and downs for every single one. We know it can get difficult at times. But know it is making you stronger and wiser. Have patience because in time it too will change. Remember the ocean waves of life we mentioned earlier. As you ride the waves of life, rising within the ocean, only to break and to roll back out to rise again, and so will you. I stretch my arms out to you. Know my love is there always.

My questions to G-d and Joshua

Me – How do I learn to trust in G-d that things will work out?

G-d - To begin with things don't always work as you desire. There is a bigger - much larger picture then you realize. But know that things will work out for the greater good. Learn to relax and know I am with you. Know in your heart I am there. Stay calm. TRUST IN YOURSELF. That is how you know I'm there for you.

The ability to trust in me starts with you. Terrible things will happen unfortunately. Reach out to me! I will listen but remember there is a bigger picture at stake and forces much larger then what you can see. Trust in me to carry you through. I will take you across the ocean if you reach out your arms. That is how you trust me.

Me – I understand how to trust but then how do I best surrender the need to control and know when I need to step in?

G-D - You will know when it is time to step in. My child you worry too much. Just relax. Control comes from the desire to be right all the time. Just relax. Great things come to those who go with the flow. You are wise and enriched with many talents. Don't worry about grabbing the reins. That is my job. What will be will be. It has been scripted out already.

Me – How much is already decided VS. free will?

G-D – You always have the power to change things. The important lesson is to remember to trust in your own instinct. Listen to the voice inside of you. Free will is a term that is miss understood. A better way to think of it is the power that is greater than all. Yes some things have been "scripted out". That is why you shouldn't stress about how things are going. The wheels are moving rest assured. Together we planned out your life before you were in the body you are in now. We planned on the lesson you need to learn. The people you need to meet or confront. Yes those things were decided.

However the power within can decide to go down a different road. Or to change the perception at which you see things. The power within has the ability to become a stronger person. For you see the mind can expand in a direction much further than you know.

That being said it is best letting things emerge as planned. So don't stress out to much. But some of that stress or power can be for your own good. If you want to feel empowered and take control of that stress than do it.

Me - If life is already scripted out, is it the little things we can change or the larger?

G-D - If it makes you feel empowered to make the big decisions than that is fine. However, know it has already been written. Yes the smaller decisions are easier for you to control. Free will is a multi-layered issue. I don't want you to sit back and not drive your life. You need to take the reins. There are more lessons to learn then what was originally planned. The power within is very strong. Hold on to that thought you do have some control.

Me – What is your thought on baptism?

G-D - It is not necessary to pledge your devotion to me Your actions take care of that. You come into this life pure. Your soul has been around many life times and sometimes it is tainted but dipping yourself in water will not release any demons you might have. That is up to you when you learn to take the reins. We bless you all when you are in the womb. It is a miracle we get you to leave the kingdom and go back to being human. That is the blessing we share with you.

Me – Do we all go to heaven?

G-D – Yes you must believe it. All my children come back to my kingdom. There are many levels here. For those who commit murder or suicide we have a "special" hospital. These souls need extra care and love. Everyone else has different levels depending on where you are in your vibrational journey. Heaven or the Kingdom is one of my favorite creations. It is miraculous. And I know all my children deserve to be here.

Think about it. Wouldn't a parent want their children to come home after being away no matter what they did well or bad? Sometimes we are not pleased with some souls and we have ways of dealing with them which we will not get into. Just trust me you are ALL welcomed.

Me – What are the best ways to show and experience love in order to protect us when life gets rough?

G-D – I would have to say one thing to start out with is believe in me or work on the love you have for yourself. A way to increase this practice is to look at a picture of yourself many times a day and say how much you love yourself. List the ways on a piece of paper. Look at the list throughout the day.

Next open a poem book about love. There are many great ones. Read these as often as possible. See me in you. When you want to feel close to me hold you hand over your heart and look in a mirror.

Another way to strengthen that wall of protection is to hear the angels sing. You can notice the songs by listening to the wind in the trees. Stop and listen to the leaves moving side to side. They make the most beautiful melody. Sometimes it is a roar. That is how the angels get your attention. But other times it is soft and gentle voices.

You can also work on compassion for others. Remember we are all on different journeys. Don't just see those who are struggling financially. Look also at those with different beliefs. They might not have the same values you have or the same struggles as you. Don't hate them. Love them for they are me.

When you are feeling down or frustrated, reach out for help. Call someone to release. And they will one day do the same for you. Community love is just as important as the love you have inside. It is impossible to feel the love all the time. You are human. There will be times you are lonely, mad or feel disrespect. And that is ok. What you do with it is what matters. You can either walk away so things don't get worse or you can smile, which I know in the heat of an argument is hard. You can also try sending your love out with your breath.

Another way is to call a friend to release. It is okay to "hash it out" as long as you end the conversations with love for the listener and for the person you are upset with. Anger or loneliness needs to be released in a constructive way.

Love takes mindfulness moments throughout the day. It is something to strive for. To just be aware, notice when you are thinking about it and when you are not. Remember to blow out the impact. Think of a pink beam of light with a red center. The color of love. Consciously blow that out.

Doing these things will build a layer of protection. Think of it as a wall of love. The stronger your barrier the better. Don't expect perfection all the time. It takes practice. Be kind to yourself!

Me – But how do we love the religions that treat women unfairly or murder children?

G-D – You love them by showing you care. Even if what they are doing is wrong. Let me handle them. That is not your job to judge. Do your best to stay out of their fire.

It is not just those you don't agree with religiously that need your help, but those you are afraid of need your compassion too. Another way to show compassion is to help the needy and the elderly. Be patient with them. Help them cross the street. I know it is easy most of the time to show compassion for them. And I know there are times when it can be difficult. Take those standing on the corner asking for money. Yes some buy alcohol or drugs instead of food, but some don't. Hear me, those lost souls struggle and need your love.

Me – What would you say to the people who struggle to find their life's purpose?

G-D – I would tell them to hold on. Take the apple that fell from the tree. It's purpose was to tempt temptation. It wasn't to land on the ground or to be eaten. Sometimes the purpose is not the act or the result but the reaction. You can all use time to reflect on your actions. Slow down and watch your step. Dig in and listen. Your purpose is to love one another and yourself. You are to learn the lesson of love and what it takes to become one. That is truly why you are here.

Me – So we shouldn't struggle to find meaningful careers?

G-d – Not exactly. It is wise to do something you enjoy and feel good about. But your true purpose is deep within.

Me – I thought people passed on when they learned all their lessons they agreed to learn?

G-D – Partly right. Before you were born we set up some goals. Once these goals are meant you choose to either stay or to return to the kingdom.

You are all here to become one and when the ego gets in the way and causes havoc, it makes it difficult to become one. Events happen as planned to "wake you up". I feel there are times when you have to learn what NOT to do. So I will create situations for you to learn from. Your question is a multi-faceted. Yes there are lessons to learn and events to observe, but your purpose is to become one with me. The only way for that to happen is to become loving. As we talked about it earlier, you must begin with yourself. Love the one you are. It sounds simpler then it is. From the time you are born parents, counselors, teachers, and care givers put negative ideas into your head. And thus it can take a life time to correct these ideas or thoughts. And that my child is my goal for you. You are more then what you feel you are. When you learn to love yourself as me, it is easier to see the love in other people or to be of service.

The illusion therefore is not the final goal but more the reality you have created.

Me – Why is it an illusion? Do we not see it and experience it?

G-D – You see it manifest from the ego. But in reality it is only there for a short time. That my child is the illusion. It doesn't last. Yes it happens but since it is not of my desire it will become dust in the wind. The only thing that survives is love.

Me – I don't understand saying it is an illusion even if it happens for a short time. It did happen. Wouldn't a better word be temporary insanity then?

Jesus – It all depends on your interpretation of illusion. Yes it actually happened. That I don't deny. What I want you to understand is that when events happen – good or bad – it doesn't matter what the outcome is if love isn't part of the equation.

Therefore a negative thing might happen but its magnitude won't last in the heart. Yes it happened, that is real but don't dwell on it. Have strength and courage and faith it will all work out in time. It is not so much as an illusion as it is faith in love.

Me – What is a good response to the question so many ask, how could G-D allow children to starve or mass murders to happen, either by man or nature?

G-D – I don't "Allow" anything to happen. Man has the power to fix their own mistakes. Humans have always been messing things up. Sometimes humans need to learn and sometimes I need to draw attention to what is wrong in order to bring about change. For instance, famine would decrease if you would lay down your weapons and concentrate more on learning to farm different types of land with different conditions. You see the answers are all there waiting for you to discover.

In terms of natural disasters they arise due to the storms in the oceans, which are partly due to climate change and partly due to my furry at what is happening in the world. I agree the two things don't mix well. My goal is wake man up. Learn to realize they have the power themselves to work together to make the world a better place.

Me – Why did Jesus agree to be baptized? I think this may confuse many and think they must do it to get to heaven.

G-D – It was more for social reasons. There were a group of followers with John the Baptist. Jesus wanted to be accepted by them. He wanted them to take him serious. So he did what they were doing. Not to be cleansed. It was more like social peer pressure. He says we all do things out of peer pressure. Not because we always believe in it. Do it if it makes you feel good. It is completely up to you.

Me – Earlier you mentioned there are false statements that have been make. What corrections can I tell people about?

G-D – The false statements are not what is necessary here. People will continue to believe as they choose. Your job is to show the world that in order to "make me happy" as you call it – we need to show them who I am and that we are creating as **one.** This a very important statement. Civilization abounds with the knowledge they are the only ones that matter. That is not true. What one does affects many. If you shoot a gun and kill a person or even an animal, the action effects many families on down the line to nature. Everyone and everything is connected. ACTIONS AFFECT ACTIONS. I can't stress this enough. I created the world as one! It is time to believe this and understand the concept. There are so many lost souls. I need you to reach out to them.

Me – Is it important for us to give tithings to succeed?

G-D – Tithings were created to get people to give of themselves. To get them to get out of their selfish ways. It makes me happy when you give to help others. However you don't need to give to a church unless that money helps other people. Communities (churches, temples, mosques etc.) are all needed for people to feel connected. But when the tithings are used for a pastor's own good, that is when I have a problem. Tithings are not supposed to make you think you have to give to receive. It doesn't work that way. You give to help others. I know what your true intention is. Help others, create a community but don't get sucked into someone's dream of becoming wealthy. Be cautious of those saying you must give to get. It is more complicated than that.

Me – How do we know when you are happy or mad?

G-D – You will know when I am happy by the sounds of earth. Listen to birds chirping or the leaves blowing in the wind. Storms are not a sign I am mad. When I'm upset you will see people angry. When I am disappointed I turn the roads upside down.

Me – Please explain that.

G-D – By that I mean road rage as you call it.

Me – Is that why we are seeing more fighting among us? What can we do to make you happier?

G-D – The increase in arguments is partly due to my disappointment with the people. However, it is also partly effect of Satan becoming stronger. Remember we are all connected as one. Your actions not only affect the person you are beating but your neighbor across the road. All emotions vibrate out.

For me to be pleased. I like to see honesty, compassion and love. These three elements are lacking. I see less and less. People go to church to hear these things preached but do them very little. Lack of honesty seems to be growing. These are the things that must change in order for the world to be as it was. I love all of you. And know you are capable of more. That is why this book is so important. I have said it before. Open your hearts and love your soul. For we are one.

In order to bring the world to a more harmonious cycle, we must learn to respect the earth and what it is capable of. Watch what you put out. Electricity, gas, drilling all effect the earth. There are better ways. Time will produce a more efficient way. Keep the intention to change alive with research.

The rules of the universe are:

1. Become aware
2. Set your intention to change
3. Take action towards the goal
4. Release all worry about the outcome. Surrender your anxiety to have these happen in your timeline. It will happen when I see fit.

In other words desire, intention, allowance, surrender.

Once you have a desire for something to occur then you make steps to make that happen. You set it in motion. You work out the details so to speak. You have your plan laid out. But don't try too hard. Allow for us to "create" together. To move the spokes of the wheel. To turn up the dust.

This is what I meant when I said earlier in the book we create together. Don't worry if it is taking too long. Surrender, trust all will happen in due time. *Believe* that is a powerful word and trust it will work out as planned.

Me - How do we get to the path of less resistant?

Joshua (Jesus) – Move into the circle of love. When you struggle or have a dilemma learn to breathe the love breath G-D mentioned earlier. Turn it over to us.

Me – Why is it so hard for humans to let go and stop trying to control?

Joshua (Jesus) – Humans think they have the power to control. When in fact they have little ability to direct the outcome. All I can say is release and let go. Stop trying so hard. Do try to make an effort. Don't give up moving in the right direction. Don't stop trying but rather stay calm don't panic. Leave the worrying to us. What will be will be. We will do the "heavy lifting so to speak". Like the saying, "don't worry".

Me – To G-D. Would you ever give up on us and disappear? Thus we would stop existing?

G-D – My child you are me and I am you. We will never stop existing. Things may get tough at times. The world as you know it may change. But we will always continue as one creation.

Me – Then you will never give up on us with floods, fires or such?

G-D – Never. I learned my lesson once before. That didn't correct anything. I may throw my wrath however.

Me – How so?

G-D – You will know by the world drastically changing. For instance, you will see day turn to night and night to day. Life will change as you know it. The sky will turn from blue to purple and only the meek will survive.

Me – What would cause you to do such a thing?

G-D – Only and only if we can't come together. That is why this book is so important. You have the power to make this world great, but so far I see so much has gone astray.

Me – If we put down our weapons and start thinking with more love and compassion will we continue as we know it?

G-D – Yes my child. That is my desire. I see so little of it. I see those in power be selfish. They look out for how much they can line their pockets or what will get more notoriety. This must change now!!!! We must learn to care about each other.

Me – If you are omnipotent and have all the power than why is there so much negative emotions or power within us? Why do we have these desires? Can't you rid these from us?

G-D – I didn't intentionally create those traits. They first emerged from the bowels of Satan.

Me – So Satan does exist? Then who created him?

G-D – Satan is a female. She came about one day when I was tired and lost control of my creations, (the birds, animals, plants everything). Satan – this wild female form arrived and has been giving me challenges after challenges.

Me – Then why don't you just get rid of her?

G-D – Once something is created they exist. My creations have just as much power as I do. We all work together. Remember this it is very important.

Me – Why is Satan female?

G-D – At the time I was working on the female form. I hadn't completed woman as we know her today. It is like a mold, an art object melting before it dried.

Me – What can we do to keep her at bay?

G-D – She only has power when you stop loving yourself, your sisters, brothers, animals and plants. She emerges every chance she gets. Keep her away by turning inside and see the joy I created WITHIN you. Then look at the beauty around. The trees, birds, water, etc. ….. Satan is getting stronger. You and only you can put her to rest.

Me – Can Satan take over our bodies?

G-D – Satin's role is to cause as much havoc as possible. She can take over your body but she also likes to cause pain. She tries to manipulate the situations to fit her needs or desires.

Me – How can we protect ourselves?

G-D – By being righteous. Satan is only as strong as you allow her to be. You have control to stop her at anytime. As a prosecutor she moves into the situation to convince you to do harm. But you have the control to dis-arm her by forcing your desires to stop. For some this is a challenge because they have been harmed as a child and know no other way. But they have the power to slow down and reconsider. The righteous will overturn and become the dominate race.

I know at times it doesn't seem so but trust in the lord (Me) and all will respond with love and respect.

Me – Are we created in your image?

G-D – No. I am light and energy. This is one of many false statements. I created man and woman to give me form. I saw early on I needed forms such as trees, animals, and man etc. to get my actions out. Now you understand, the world is all me and thus you are me.

Me – Do you get lonely knowing you are the only one who exists in light and energy?

G-D – That is how I knew I needed at least two of everything.

Me – Do you have emotions?

G-D – Not as you experience them. That is something I created for you to learn to expand and grow. I do feel things and experience ups and downs as you would know it. But it is different for me. I'm more like a dog who wags its tail when he is happy. Thus, my energy glows more when I'm happy. And darkens when I am disappointed.

Me – What about the changes we are seeing in the earth and atmosphere?

G-D – Your use of fossil fuels is alarming. You must find an alternative. Global warming exists and it is changing the planet – my creation. There are alternatives that exist. You haven't discovered them yet but will in time. Keep putting forth the effort to find new ways to move your cars and to see light. There are other possibilities.

Me – Should we show love to mother earth? Is that the correct term?

G-D – The correct term is me. My earth, my trees, my oceans etc. … Love would help but new discoveries are just as important. Yes emotions help but it is more involved than that. Look to the earth for help for the changes in temperature to slow the warming.

Me – Are you talking about use of crystals, metals, gas or some other renewable source?

G-D – Possibly. The power is within your scientist.

Me – I just want to be clear. We haven't discovered the solution yet?

G-D – Not yet. And it may be a combination of several. So don't scrap what you have already worked on.

Me – It seems like in today's atmosphere there is so much hate and people cheating each other. Is this your way of being upset?

G-D – No my child the beatings, killings, lying and cheating is do more to the despair of the world. Yes, I am upset about this. But know my wrath comes in waves. You will know I'm upset when the ocean waves rise when no storms are around. Or the trees bend when the wind rises. You will know I'm upset when you hear me roar. I show this by hurling fire bombs and wicked storms. Not by humans going wild. That is completely on you.

Me – I'm confused. I thought you said that when nature takes out a town this was not you showing your disappointment?

G-D – I need to explain better. I see your confusion. I do show my distain at times with the weather but my display has more to do with a storm coming out from nowhere. Not something the weather people have picked up on their radars days in advance. When you see planned storms that is due to the atmospheric changes. Not me. I don't show you my disappointment to often that is why you probably are not aware of the few times it did happen.

Me – But you said earlier since we are one, we will see other people getting mad when it is you who is upset?

G-D – Yes and no. Anger vibrates out and affects others, me included. However my anger that shows itself through humans is more like a fan that waves and then cracks and thus stops working. So when you see angry people it is partly me but more them reacting to something.

Me – Then are these the people that seem to do something drastic?

G-D – No my child. The negative emotions are more about the person's anger or fear. That is not me.

Me – I'm so confused. I understood you to have said earlier that road rage was you showing us your disappointment in us?

G-D – Ah I see. You are getting hung up on the term road rage. I suppose I didn't explain myself well. I should have explained it more like an unexplained desire to do erratic behavior. This doesn't present itself very often. That is why I shouldn't have explained it the way I did earlier.

Me – So when we see things that can't be explained in the weather or maybe one of our emotions, it is really you?

G-D – Yes now you are getting it.

Me – Will you tell me next time it does happen?

G-D – Yes you will know. I promise you that.

Me – Does sin separate us?

G-D – Sin has many levels as you can imagine. But we are all one and thus cannot separate ourselves. Even the worse sinners are stuck with the purest. Together we rise. The yin and yang so to speak. Together as one.

You are inclined to do well. The power of Satin is only as strong as you allow her to be.

Me – Going back to the creation of time. Why did you decide to create humans and is there only one couple that started us all?

G-D – Back in the beginning of time. I created dinosaurs, animals and nature. But I soon realized I needed something else. Thus man was created and a partner to reproduce. Yes one couple created everyone else. Humans emerged around the world quickly by travel or roaming the earth as you would call it. Adam and Eve as you have called them are truly the parents of every human. You are all family true and true. Take no harm in this. Not one race is better than the other. We are all together as equals.

Me – Is Jesus our savior?

G-D – He is not. I created Jesus to help the sinners of the world know they are loved and to be my voice for change and truth.

Me – Did Jesus really say at the last super to drink the wine as his blood?

Jesus – I meant for people to understand when I pass that I am still with them. Just like wine that keeps on flowing, so do I. I wanted my teachings of love and respect to carry on. I didn't want anyone to forget once I was "gone".

Me – Jesus did you say you are the way?

Jesus – No I never said that. That too got misinterpreted. I'm not sure how that got started but I can only surmise it started when I said this is the way G-D wants us to be. Meaning – loving, kind, caring and compassionate. Not evil or lying your way to the top. G-D created us to be as one (like him). Meaning to look out for each other. To help each other when we are down not to squash our brothers and sisters.

Me – It seems as humans, we all strive for prosperity. What is the best way to have all we want?

G-D – Prosperity is a frame of mind. But if you are talking about material objects I would say work hard and trust in me the Lord. It seems to be in your "DNA" to want things. Not everyone needs to be rich to feel prosperity. I give you what you need to learn from. Objects don't create wealth. People do. Yes you need to pay bills and keep a roof over your head. Learn to create new things, work hard, do your best and surrender to me. Things will come to those in need.

The universe will deliver to those who have love. However, if you insist on having something tangible. Practice the thought of what you want in your mind. Picture it and feel what it would be like to have the item you want. Depending on your space in time we will grant what you want. It really depends on if this thing you so desire is best for you right now.

Me – Why are there hurricanes, tornados, earthquakes, fires and tsunamis that bring such damage?

G-D – Huge natural disasters are a sign of things to come if we don't change. I'm giving you a taste of what will be.

Me – Is this how we know you are upset or disappointed.

G-D – Yes and no. Yes I create the storms but that is not my wrath. That is shown in different ways. Natural disasters are partly due to climate change and it is also due to my desire to see change in the world. It seems these bring out the best in mankind. I want you to know you are capable of kindness, of leaving your valuables behind and focusing on love. That my child is what we need more of.

Me – Then climate change is real and we need to work on it?

G-D – Yes of course it is. The ozone is definitely affected by your fumes from your automobiles and the current omitted from the electricity, oil, and gas. Together they are not a good combination.

Take the road ahead. Smell the air as it is now it will not be the same down the road if things don't change now! You are not separate from the wilderness. Remember, we are all one and that includes nature. What effects humans also has a bearing on the forest and sky. And thus if the wildlife gets hurt so do you. There is no separation between nature and man.

Me – Was Jesus (Joshua) resurrected?

G-D – He was in terms of his soul came to say good bye to his wife Mary. Not too many were able to see his image however. There were a few other women around her when it happened. She only heard his voice. At that time he no longer had a body. So if you call that a resurrected then yes. Everyone is capable of coming back to say goodbye. They choose not to because it will disturb their love ones. Those who believe in life after death will understand.

Me – Please explain life after death. I think it would be helpful for others.

G-D – Life after death is a term used for those who believes in the never ending life of the soul.

Jesus didn't come back as he was when he was human but as a spirit of himself.

Jesus – I was not resurrected. The people who say they saw me did so to better their desire to advance their beliefs. I came to Mary in voice to say I was alright and in a happy beautiful place. That is all I did.

It is unfortunate that people made up lies to better their place in history. Believe me when I say it did NOT happen. I know this will come as a shock to most. I am sorry you believed what didn't happen for so long. That is unfortunate but it is time the truth needs to be revealed.

Me to G-d – Why did you have Joshua (Jesus) pass on so early?

G-D – As I mentioned earlier. I knew he would be of more help here by my side. He did what he could there as a human and it was time for him to move on.

Me – Are there manuscripts that prove he is your son?

G-D – You are all my sons and daughters. Yes, I asked him to do my work. To help those heal and who were sick and to spread my teachings of love and compassion. There are times I need human aid and need to call upon those who can hear me. Much like the work in this book.

Me – To Joshua - You gave up your family when you knew you were going to be crucified. Why?

Joshua – Yes it was the ultimate sacrifice. G-D or father Aba as I prefer to say, told me what would happen. So yes I was prepared but not for the pain. It was very painful. But I knew it had to be done for mankind. I didn't know other religions would emerge from it but I did know it would give people hope. I had to think of the larger picture of society then just my family. They paid the real price. They had to go on without me.

Me – You could have taught people so much more as a human though.

Joshua – Not true. I have been continuing teaching people through the Course in Miracles and in The Way of Mastery. These books have reached many people.

Me – Yes in the present day but what about back in your human time?

Joshua – Only a select few wanted to hear. I did what I could at the time. There were many more that were fearful of me. I only wanted to show them Aba's love but they couldn't hear what I could hear from father and thus deemed me crazy. I tell you this because there are forces not all can see, touch, understand or hear. But trust me they do exist. I am not special. But I trust in father and do as he commands me to do.

I laid on the cross to remind people to remember my teachings and to pray for a better life of love and compassion. That is what we want for all of you. Trust in our Lord our G-D. Be the power of thy spirit. Amen.

Me – Some people believe in an omnipotent G-D. What would you say to those who want to understand your power?

G-D – I am the all-encompassing powerful G-D. However, I also have limits to my greatness. To those who want to believe I can do all, create all, be all - you are wrong. My powers can take me to the end of time. However, you are capable of many things I am not. You have physical form to adjust objects. I cannot. A voice that can be heard. You have hands and feet. I do not. And thus I need you. For we "create" together. I can make mountains move but you can make knives move. I can save lives by adjusting your thoughts when you listen. But you can save lives by working together. You have a saying, "It takes a village to raise a child" and it takes a village to make the world go around smoothly. You see we need each other on many levels. I can only do so much.

Me – How can we study our past if we all believe in something different? I'm asking so we can all come together.

G-D – You should know what your heritage was long ago. History is important. Yes my child, but let it go at that. History is just that. The past of long ago. Tell the people to focus on the now. The present moment.

Me – Is there human life on other planets?

G-D – Most definitely. You are not the only humans in the galaxy. The other planets are more advance then you. They have visited earth many times. There will be a time in the future that you will meet but that is way down the road.

The other lives are afraid of your anger. When we can control that more they will show themselves to you. When you do meet stay calm. They do not look like you and are here to do you no harm. They are a gentle people.

Me – What do you think of the mindfulness revolution? Can it change the way people behave?

G-D – This my child is a long answer but here is the short of it. Mindfulness has a place in the world as we know it. It needs to be respected on many levels.

First of all for the cognitive mind, the awareness of the now. To seek the awareness of why you are feeling the way you are. This is a good thing. But go deeper much deeper. Harness that power of calmness. Go further into the mind. Take the awareness on a journey around the globe. Look at your feelings as well as the emotions of your fellow man. Then stretch it out to awareness of your block or county. Then stretch it to your city. Then to your state and then to your country. Now bring your awareness down on planet earth. See all the people rushing around. Tell yourself that is NOT YOU. You are here. Inside your magnificent body which I created. Rest and breath.

Now remember the power of love. Breathe that in. Stop the chatter and smell the roses. Be at one with me. Mindfulness is just the tip of the bird.

Me – What else should we know about this then?

Why is it important to view our neighborhood and through our planet earth for mindfulness appreciation?

G-D – It is important to view the people around you just as it is important as it is to focus on yourself. And realize that we need each other to survive. By bringing your focus out allows you to shift your awareness to others whom may be in need. Your shift brings them energy that you cannot see with your naked eye. To keep the earth revolving we must realize our connectedness. It is important to understand the self AND the world in which you are currently living.

Me – Why are we here?

G-D – You are here to experience life on many different levels. One, be aware of the now, the present. Two, we have brought you into this dimension to learn how to "roll with it". To destress, come to a place of surrender. Let me work my magic and create the life you desire. And three, to love and respect one another. To find the compassion you all long for. I created this mess but I need each and every one of you to get us out.

Me – Would you like us to put down our religious beliefs and come together?

G-D – Yes of course, that is our goal. To unite. To see love in us all. Religion is good for history but we are in a time of change and that change is the present. A time that communities need to focus on the now. The present time. Not a time of long ago. This is a time of unrest. A lot of tremendous turmoil. Without the power of love and empathy you cannot survive in a world as you know it. You must react NOW! Time is short. Be as one.

Me – You have mentioned honoring our parents. My question to you is why? Especially when so many parents have harmed their kids.

G-D – Parents don't intentionally harm their offspring. They were brought up that way. It was out of their control. They had no way of knowing what is right and what is wrong.

By honoring your parents you become as one with the one that created you. Understand their lack of knowledge. For they know not. Forgiveness grows your heart and makes you more powerful and brings you closer to the power of the light within.

Me – What did Jesus mean when he said you will inherit the Kingdom of heaven?

Jesus – I meant all mankind will live in a place of greatness when they learn to love one another. The gospels changed my true intentions. We are all creatures of love. We just don't show it. The Kingdom of Heaven is the magical place of beauty, wisdom and clarity. This I know is so because I live it every day.

You are the one who will bring the Kingdom of G-D to the people to achieve peace. The Kingdom is there for everyone who believes and holds us in their hearts. In order to belong to the Kingdom you must trust in us. The Kingdom brings peace when you are down. It brings love to those who fear they have none. It brings prosperity to those who feel they lack. You just have to surrender and the Kingdom will be there.

Me – Did you die for our sins Jesus?

Jesus – I died for you to learn mercy, compassion and love. What you do in your own life is on you and no one else. We are not inherently sinners. Yes no one is perfect but the base of all your souls is bliss – pure love. Every one of you is created for great things. Learn to trust in the Great Almighty. When you stray from wishes of greatness you leave behind a trail of destruction.

Me – Was Joshua born from a virgin?

G-D – He was not. He came to be just like every human. From a man and a woman.

Me – Was Joshua (Jesus) born in Bethlehem?

G-D – He was not. And he was not born in a manger. He was born at his parents' house in a bed of straw. That is how they birthed the babies back then. There was never a creed for all to go to Bethlehem to file their taxes. That was false story.

Me – Did Joshua change water into wine at a wedding?

G-D – That he did with my help. I wanted the people to believe his teachings.

Me – Did he heal those inflected with Leprosery?

G-D – Yes again with my help.

Me – Did he walk on water?

G-D – He did with the help of many rocks and a few angels holding him up. He needed to rescue some men who were drowning. Swimming out to them was out of the question at that time.

Jesus wasn't prepared to swim that distance. He came to me for help. That is what prayer can do.

Me – Is the shroud of Taren real?

G-D – It is a fake. An artist friend of Joshua was upset with what had happened to him. The artist painted it to honor his friendship. The cloth came from the Pharisee. He too felt guilty at what had happened to Joshua.

Me – Then how did the art on the cloth become dimensional?

G-D – The machine that measured the authenticity of the cloth is not accurate. Trust me when I say it is a painting and nothing else.

Me – Do you want us to worship you?

G-D – That is up to every individual. I will love you no matter what you do. Keep in mind I hear your prayers along with your thoughts. So just by thinking I hear you. And know what your intentions are. That is truly how I understand what is evolving in your minds.

Me – you mentioned to put down our idols. I thought we have. Can you explain exactly what you desire?

G-D – No my child. It would cause too much pain for some. If an idol will make them feel love and self-worth so be it. I would prefer for your prayers to be directed at me and not some piece of metal, however. Please understand I am with you always.

Me – G-D what do you want to say to people who ask why are there disease and mass shootings? What could possibly be a reason for these monstrosities?

G-D – My child you can't begin to understand the reasons behind many things. For one disease is a way to purge the negative thoughts you create. Change those thoughts and the world will change with you. On the other side, be those thoughts and force the world into casualties. Love heals all wounds both physical and mentally. Disease is a warning light. A message to wake up and smell the roses as you say. I needed something to get your attention and mortality always works.

Disease is also a way to get you to move on. I needed a way to transpire a new transition. A place where you can say good bye to the old and hello to the new.

In terms of major monstrosities I would say patience. It is a complicated issue. Mass shootings are not my work. They are the signature of Satan. She takes over. I wish people didn't get hurt. But unfortunately they do. I'm working on reducing the effects of Satan but it is a multi-faceted problem.

One being Satan and two the lack of love in the world causes the amount of causalities. Remember LOVE conquers all! It is the glue that holds the world together. The more love and compassion the less Satan has power over you.

The shootings and bombings will continue to increase till you as a people of LOVE change! That is why this is SO important. I am begging you to change!! Things can be better but the power is in you! Don't let Satan win! Be the glue. Show her love. Take the world in your hands. I know you can do it now! Not later. Each and every one of you has the power to keep the sky blue and the grass green. If not things will only get worse. Be strong, be kind, and be honest. That is my desire.

Me – Is there anything we can do to stop these senseless events?

G-D – What I truly desire is love one another. These shootings are coming at a time of much distress. A time of conflict everywhere. In order for peace to abound you must be at peace within. I know you are wondering about those with mental problems, and yes that is a concern. But you must understand these individuals are upset. They have lost their faith in me and those around them. In order to stop the killings every one of you must first believe in me and then trust in the holy spirit of love.

Me – But what if their mental stability doesn't allow them the latitude for this to happen?

G-D – They will if they would reach out to us. I hear your cry for gun control and yes that would help but even more so is a lack of universal love and connection with spirit. We can help those who ask. This is the problem. Many don't know we love them and therefore they have lost their way.

Me to Joshua – In the Course of Miracles you mentioned desire and the effects it has on us both positive and negative. Can you speak on that please?

Joshua – Desire comes from the ego. The desire to be. The desire to have. The desire to control. The desire to hurt someone. The desire to attach false emotions either to yourself or someone else. Be thy will means set your intention and release. Give your power over to us. Let go of your ego. Change your perspective. Too much wealth can only hurt someone. Have the desire to accomplish goals. Set your intention but then RELAX.

However, if you are talking about desire to hurt yourself or someone else STOP. Know we are created as one. You will affect other people whom did nothing. Plus, you will affect nature. No one should ever wish harm on anyone. The repercussion goes much further then you are aware. There is never a right side or wrong side. But rather many places in between. Take this negative desire and walk away when it does not come from love.

Close that circle of doubt by trusting in the Almighty. Fear, jealousy, callousness, these are all qualities of lack thereof. If you are fearful something will arise. Watch those thoughts for you will create them.

Jealousy, loneliness, callous can be corrected with knowing you are loved. And you are the best you can be at this time. Don't expect perfection. That cannot be. There must be many lessons to learn before that happens. When you know you have us inside, you can't be lonely. However, we know humans need humans and when the time is right companionship will come forth. Trust in the lord. He will take you far.

Those who doubt so badly that they become callous are the most fearful. They don't see all they do have and thus become so fearful and ashamed they lose their power of love. These people are so driven by their egos they can't see beyond themselves. They must step back and see what they do have. Find their internal love of themselves. This is the only way they "fix" what is wrong.

Doubt and desire can go unnoticed till something bad happens. Suddenly they will awaken. Hopefully it won't be too late for their current life.

Me to G-D – I can hear you but for those who can't, how do they know you are around?

G-D – You know I'm here when your heart beats. When you look outside and see the sun, the trees, and the wind blowing. That is all a part of me. You know I'm near when you sense a change in the air. When you suddenly smell something that wasn't there before. Open your eyes and see. Open your sense of smell. This is me. You have to trust in order to believe.

I know that is the hard part for many to believe in me. In order to become one, look around you, feel and sense we belong together. Feel me. Trust in me. My desire is for more of you to believe. That I would truly like.

"Trust in the Lord for he who knows you will succeed. For I am the Lord thy G-D. Amen"

Me – I have a history question. Did you really take a rib from Adam to make a woman? And if you have all the power, why did you want Adam and Eve to be tempted in Garden of Eden? Why not just have them procreate without the mention of temptation?

G-D – First part about Adam and the rib. That is a story made up. I never needed a rib to create Eve. She came to being solely on my own creation. I created woman so man wasn't alone and had a companion.

Next part of the question concerning temptation. This was the beginning of free will. Yes I knew they would choose the apple. And they would have gotten pregnant no matter what they chose. But I wanted them to make the decision and feel they were in charge of their destiny. Much like I do to you today. You have the power to create the life you want. The serpent is always around tempting you to choose one way or another. Certain actions don't change. Only the outcome or reaction which has to do with the times and your desire. In other words, I will always give you a temptation to go down two paths, the choice will always be up to you and that is exactly what Adam and Eve experienced.

This is why history matters but is not what should rule your life. Learn from other people's mistakes so you can make an informed decision. I am not saying Adam and Eve made a mistake. Do not read more into what I'm saying. I am trying to bring the lesson into the present. That is all I'm conveying about the lesson of the past.

Me – I'm finally understanding our brokenness. The lack of compassion for other perspectives. We have lost sight of the ability to reason or understand difference of opinions. It seems that most feel it is their way not their neighbor's way which is correct. And nothing in between is possible. We are all different which makes things interesting and allows our unique values to shine. I have seen some friends who want to do away with the people that don't agree with them. That makes us no different than Hitler.

I'm finally getting it. We see what we want to see. We close all doors that should be open. A door that lets our beliefs be viewed without attacking. Not all differences are due to color, religion, race or politics but also opinions. Where is the mercy? The ability to live life in harmony? I see such hatred.

G-D – My child I am proud of you. Now you see and feel the pain I have. It is not just about love but understanding of everyone's right to be who they truly are and to be accepted. The world is so broken!! We must show the ability to unite in the face of diversity.

Let me be clear. Yes we need gun control. I know it is on your mind and yes we need a forum to discuss our differences without attacking. A place to join hands. A place to embrace one another.

It doesn't matter whose way is right but rather a way to compromise. Money and power has always been at the crust of it. That will never change my child. However if you can raise awareness to the possibility of compromise, that is my dream and your goal. A place you can allow your differences to be heard. A place that is calm and peaceful. A place where money or power doesn't exist. A round table as such. That is what is needed.

This is the direction you need to take my child. My blessings to you.

Me – Are we at a time of rapture and the anti-Christ? There was a prophecy of one central government. Will this come to be?

G-D – Yes my child the days of life as you are used to are near an end. There will be a massive war between two kingdoms which will ensure a change for the rest of the countries.

Unfortunately, the time is near. A time of much unrest. You will see fires like non other seen as of yet. Some leaders will perish. One nation under G-D will exist. Then and only then will you truly understand we are one.

Me – Who is the anti-Christ and what does that mean?

G-D – The anti-Christ will set the story straight. A person that will tell the truth and dispel the lies that have been told in the bible. The anti-Christ is full of love and understanding. A maternal nurturing female. A person that will show the world what true devotion really is.

Me – Who will emerge as our leader? Will it be someone from this country?

G-D – The boundaries of countries will merge. The leaders will be many. Not one but more of a team.

I am not trying to frighten you but prepare you for a time like no other. A time that will have much beauty, just in a different way.

Me – Why does this need to happen?

G-D – To clear the way for a different type of society. A society of followers of my correct word. There is still much to be discovered. I want people to understand when the dust settles that a better time will be near. A time when people will pull together with honesty and support.

As you know these are times that are very volatile. Conflict is everywhere. Negative vibrations are winning out over positive ones. People are arguing over smallest things. It isn't just about race anymore. Yes that is part of it. More importantly it is more about defeating anyone that doesn't think the same and completely removing them from this lifetime. The vibration right now is very low.

In order to bring things back to a higher vibration we need to make major changes on this path of destruction. This path I am speaking about is twofold. One that each and every one of you are creating. The thoughts of "my way is the ONLY correct way." There is no middle ground with you.

Please hear my words. This must end NOW!

The second part of destruction is between countries. There are many countries with problems but for our purpose here I am talking about the US and Russia. These countries will become even bigger enemies then they are now. Those in charge on both sides want complete power. They think they are working together but in fact they are not. The rife between them will only get worse before it succumbs. All I can tell you is there will **not** be a major war with many lives at risk but rather a breakdown of governing powers.

My blessings to all. I know everyone can and will become as one, with love and compassion growing all around.

Amen

Printed in the United States
By Bookmasters